New Estimates of the Effect of Kassebaum-Kennedy's Group-to-Individual Conversion Provision on Premiums for Individual Health Insurance

Jacob Alex Klerman

Prepared for the United States Department of Labor

RAND

PREFACE

Using new tabulations from the Survey of Income and Program Participation (SIPP) and newly released data from the Current Population Survey (CPS), this report reexamines the likely effect of the Health Insurance Act of 1995 (commonly known as "Kassebaum-Kennedy") on insurance premiums for individuals purchasing health insurance in the individual health insurance market. A widely cited study by the Health Insurance Association of America (HIAA) estimates that the proposed legislation would increase premiums for those currently buying individual health insurance by over 20 percent. The present report finds a much smaller increase, estimating a range of effects from 5.7 percent to under 1 percent. The upper end of the range maintains the HIAA assumptions but substitutes new tabulations (from SIPP and CPS) of the figures used in the computation of the estimate. The lower end of the range considers the interaction of the proposed federal legislation with current state insurance regulations.

This report was funded by the Pension and Welfare Benefits Administration, U.S. Department of Labor, as part of RAND's Center for the Study of Employee Health Benefits. It will be of interest to those considering programs to raise the level of health insurance coverage in the United States.

CONTENTS

TABLES

SUMMARY

One provision of the Health Insurance Reform Act of 1995 (S. 1028, sponsored by Senators Kassebaum and Kennedy) would guarantee the right to convert a terminating group health insurance policy into an individual health insurance policy. The Health Insurance Association of America (HIAA) has opposed this "conversion" provision, estimating that it would raise health insurance premiums in the individual market by 22.1 percent (HIAA's "most likely" long-term estimate). However, the analyses of this report suggest much smaller effects, and, therefore imply less reason to oppose the proposed legislation's conversion provision.

We use the HIAA analysis structure and assumptions but substitute new tabulations from the Survey of Income and Program Participation (SIPP) and improved estimates based on newly released, improved Current Population Survey (CPS) data. The resulting estimates of potential increases range from 5.7 percent to under 1 percent. The highest estimate maintains all of the HIAA assumptions but substitutes improved values for some of the key figures. The lowest estimate, under 1 percent, uses alternative assumptions about how states will regulate these conversion policies and the likely claim costs of those buying the conversion coverage.

WHY THE DIFFERENCE IN ESTIMATES?

Under the proposed Health Insurance Reform Act of 1995, job leavers who have been continuously covered under a group health insurance plan for 18 months—and who do not have access to any other group health insurance—would be guaranteed the right to purchase individual health insurance from any health insurance company offering such insurance in that state. For job leavers from firms with 20 or more employees, this conversion right would take effect after an individual exhausted continuation coverage under the Consolidated Omnibus Budget Reconciliation Act of 1986 (COBRA), usually 18 months after leaving a job. For job leavers from firms with fewer than 20 employees—who are not eligible for COBRA—the conversion right would take effect when an individual leaves the job.

The HIAA opposes this conversion provision, claiming that over the long term it would raise insurance premiums for people currently in the individual health insurance market by 22.1 percent. This estimate assumes that individuals purchasing conversion policies would have claims double those of individuals currently purchasing individual health insurance policies. Furthermore, it assumes that these higher costs would be spread evenly over all participants in the individual health insurance market; that is to say, it assumes *pure community rating* in the individual insurance market.

Given these assumptions, to project the effect of the conversion policies, an analyst needs estimates of (1) the number of covered lives currently in the individual health insurance market and (2) the number of newly covered lives in that market resulting from conversion policies. Table S.1 shows how the HIAA methodology estimates the number of additional covered lives resulting from the proposed conversion right. The estimate combines separate computations for the COBRA market (firms with 20 or more employees) and the sub-COBRA market (firms with fewer than 20 employees). For each market, the subtotal ("total insured years") is the product of the first four rows of the table.

The "HIAA-RAND" estimate maintains the HIAA analysis structure and assumptions but uses newly released CPS data and new tabulations from the SIPP. These new figures are preferable to those used by HIAA for several reasons:

- First, our population estimates ("covered lives") are based on 1995 CPS data that have been released since the original HIAA analysis. Beyond being more current, these new CPS data are based on a new battery of CPS health insurance questions

Table S.1

Premium Effects: Original HIAA Estimates and RAND Estimates

	HIAA		HIAA-RAND		RAND-Best	
	COBRA	Sub-COBRA	COBRA	Sub-COBRA	COBRA	Sub-COBRA
Covered lives (in millions)	120.0	30.0	124.5	13.2	124.5	13.2
Percentage leaving job (per year)	12.0%	20.0%	16.6%	24.6%	16.6%	24.6%
Percentage of job leavers eligible for the program	4.0%	100.0%	0.8%	88.3%	0.8%	88.3%
Insured years per eligible person	2.00	0.30	2.00	0.11	2.00	0.11
Total insured years (in millions)	1.15	1.80	0.31	0.32	0.31	0.32
Ratio of claims costs of new policies to those of current policies	200%	200%	200%	200%	150%	150%
Current insured years (in millions)	10.4		10.4		13.1	
Increase in average premium	22.1%		5.7%		2.3%	

NOTE: HIAA figures are derived from *The Cost of Ending "Job Lock" or How Much Would Health Insurance Costs Go Up If "Portability" of Health Insurance Were Guaranteed? Preliminary Estimates—July 26, 1995,* Washington, D.C.: HIAA, 1995.

specifically redesigned to improve the measurement of health insurance status.

- Second, while HIAA used only what data were available from published sources for job turnover rates (shown in the table as "percentage leaving job"), the SIPP tabulations that we used were computed specifically to analyze the proposed legislation. As far as possible, the concepts used in these tabulations are the appropriate ones for the analysis of conversion coverage.

- Third, HIAA's estimates for the length of time people currently spend on COBRA and the share of people exhausting COBRA (used in the table to estimate the "percentage of job leavers eligible for the program" and "insured years per eligible person") are based on a small number of survey responses from an unrepresentative sample of employers. Our figures are based on the

SIPP, a nationally representative probability sample conducted by the U.S. Bureau of the Census.

Using these newer, more specific CPS and SIPP figures, the center panel of the table (labeled "HIAA-RAND") recomputes the HIAA estimate. This HIAA-RAND estimate implies that premiums in the individual insurance market would rise by 5.7 percent—about a quarter of the HIAA estimate of 22.1 percent.

WHY THE CONVERSION EFFECT MIGHT BE EVEN LOWER

The "HIAA-RAND" estimate of 5.7 percent deliberately follows the HIAA analysis, except where we have used new tabulations (from CPS and SIPP data) to suggest more appropriate or more accurate estimates. The right panel of the table (labeled "RAND-Best") recomputes the HIAA estimate and adjusts two assumptions about the most likely effects of the proposed legislation:

- First, the RAND-Best estimate assumes that the new conversion policies will be pooled not only with those that are currently regulated as individual policies, but also with policies that are sold like individual policies (even though they may not currently be regulated as such). This increases the estimate of the number of the current insured years from 10.4 million to 13.1 million.

- Second, while HIAA assumes that claim costs for the conversion policies will be much higher (200 percent higher) than those for current group insurance claims, the RAND-Best estimate assumes that claim costs for conversion policies will be similar to the claim costs of people currently insured under COBRA (150 percent of individual rates).

With these two assumptions, our study's best estimate of the effect of the legislation—in states with perfect community rating (which is the HIAA assumption)—is only 2.3 percent.

However, there is strong reason to believe that even these estimates are much too high. The HIAA methodology estimates the "aggregate additional cost that would be imposed on the individual insurance market." That would be the effect on the premiums for people currently purchasing individual health insurance—but only if conversion coverage policies are priced in a pure community-rated pool together with existing individual policies. Nothing in the proposed legislation prevents insurance companies from treating the new conversion policies as a separate rating pool. If insurance companies did so, there would be *absolutely no premium increase* for those currently buying individual health insurance.

Both the proposed legislation and HIAA's analysis note the crucial role of state regulation in the individual health insurance market. Many states already provide—either directly or through high-risk pools—some form of guaranteed issue rights similar to the conversion rights guaranteed by the proposed legislation. Because passage of the federal legislation will not increase the number of policies or the cost of policies in these states, the estimates should not be applied to individuals living there. Furthermore, most states currently impose no rate restrictions on individual premiums. In those states, insurance companies could treat conversion policies as a separate rating pool. Thus, in those states there would also be no effect on health insurance rates for those currently buying individual health insurance.

Finally, even in those states that now regulate individual health insurance premiums (or those that might chose to do so if the proposed legislation becomes law), the regulation does not require a single rate but limits the *range of rates* in the individual markets. On the premiums of those currently purchasing individual health insurance, such limits would also imply an effect considerably smaller than that implied by even the RAND-Best estimate presented in Table S.1.

Thus, plausible increases in premiums for those currently purchasing individual health insurance would range from 5.7 percent to under 1 percent. The upper end of the range maintains the HIAA assumption of pooling costs between those currently purchasing individual insurance and the new conversion policies. The lower end of the range assumes the continuation of current state insurance regulations. The most plausible estimate is toward the lower end. Moreover, the phase-in period of this long-run estimate would be several years. Since the individual health insurance market has had recent premium increases well over 5 percent per year, the long-run effect of this legislation would likely be undetectable.

The original HIAA estimate of premium increases of over 20 percent for those currently buying health insurance in the individual health insurance market understandably induced many to reconsider the desirability of such a conversion right. By comparison, our preferred range of estimates of 5.7 percent to under 1 percent suggests that likely premium increases for those currently buying health insurance in the individual insurance market provide less reason to oppose the proposed legislation.

ACKNOWLEDGMENTS

This report has benefited from conversations with my colleagues in the RAND Center for the Study of Employee Health Benefits: Joan Buchanan, Pam Short, Steve Long, and Arleen Leibowitz. Joyce Peterson, Emmett Keeler, and Rebecca Kilburn of RAND improved both the content and the presentation.

The apparently simple tabulations reported here represent major programming efforts of Sally Carson and Roald Euller. Together they have successfully wrestled with the unruly SIPP data. The preparation of the manuscript was ably assisted by J. Natasha Kostan, Edie Nichols, and Jana Otto.

LIST OF ACRONYMS AND ABBREVIATIONS

AAA	American Academy of Actuaries
BCBS	BlueCross BlueShield Association
COBRA	Consolidated Omnibus Budget Reconciliation Act of 1986
CPS	Current Population Survey
GAO	General Accounting Office
GI	Guaranteed issue
HIAA	Health Insurance Association of America
HRP	High-risk pool
IND	Current participants in the individual health insurance market
K-K	Health Insurance Reform Act of 1995 (S. 1028, sponsored by Senators Kassebaum and Kennedy)
NAIC	National Association of Insurance Commissioners
RR	Rate regulation
SIPP	Survey of Income and Program Participation

Chapter One

INTRODUCTION

To increase the level of health insurance coverage in the United States, the proposed Health Insurance Reform Act of 1995 (S. 1028, sponsored by Senators Kassebaum and Kennedy) would limit the ability of insurers or employers to impose preexisting-condition limitations on health insurance coverage and would require that insurers offer health insurance to anyone who has been continuously enrolled in a group health insurance plan for 18 months or more. This latter "group-to-individual conversion" provision (hereafter simply "conversion coverage") has been strongly opposed by the health insurance industry's trade organization, the Health Insurance Association of America (HIAA). HIAA claims that passage of the provision will increase health insurance premiums of those currently buying individual insurance by over 20 percent.

POSSIBLE EFFECTS OF THE PROPOSED LEGISLATION

This report explores the likely effects of the proposed legislation in three steps.

- The first step notes that the key figures used in the HIAA computations were based on available published statistics. However, the appropriate figures were often not available in published source. Instead, HIAA was forced to use not precisely appropriate figures or the figures were from selected (nonrepresentative) samples. This first step maintains the basic HIAA analytic structure and assumptions but substitutes new figures based on new tabulations from nationally representative data collected by the U.S. Bureau of the Census.

In some cases, we substitute recently released (since the original HIAA analysis) figures from HIAA's original source, the Current Population Survey (CPS). The CPS is a large annual nationally representative survey conducted by the U.S. Bureau of the Census. In addition to being more current, these recently released data incorporate revised batteries of questions that were explicitly designed to improve the measurement of key quantities in the HIAA analysis.

In other cases, since the appropriate published tabulations were not available, HIAA used tabulations from nonrepresentative insurance industry sources or other published tabulations of related concepts (but not necessarily for a recent period or for the appropriate subpopulations). Our estimates use new appropriately designed tabulations from the Survey of Income and Program Participation (SIPP). The SIPP is a large nationally representative probability sample of the U.S. population conducted by the U.S. Bureau of the Census. It collects extensive information on health insurance coverage and employment status on a sample of people it follows for more than a two-year period. Using the individual-level data, we have tailored our tabulations as much as possible to the details of the proposed legislation.

- The second step maintains the basic structure of the HIAA approach but alters HIAA assumptions about what will be treated as an "individual policy" and the relative claim costs of these conversion policies.

- The third step questions the applicability of the HIAA methodology. The proposed federal legislation has no restrictions on premiums. Thus, except for state insurance regulation, insurance companies could set separate premiums for the conversion policies mandated by the proposed federal legislation to cover their own claims. In that case, the proposed legislation would have no effect on the premiums of those currently buying individual insurance.

The HIAA analysis makes the opposite assumption—that insurance companies would increase current individual premiums proportionately to the increase in average claims induced by the proposed federal legislation. No state's current legislation would require such behavior. Currently most states do not in any way regulate individual health insurance premiums. Among those states that do not already require that insurance companies sell individual insurance to anyone, those that do regulate premiums allow the premiums to vary with the age of the individual and (at least to some extent) with other factors including proxies for likely claims cost.

While HIAA estimates a long-range effect of over 20 percent; our estimate is much lower. Our first step—better estimates of the underlying figures—yields a conservative (probably too high) estimate of only 5.7 percent. Our second step—adjusting two of the assumptions to what we believe are more plausible values, yields an estimate of 2.3 percent. Our third step implies that in most states the effect will be zero and that in those states in which it is not zero, it will be only a fraction of even our second step estimate of 2.3 percent.

PLAN OF THE REPORT

Chapter Two presents a discussion of the problems in the health insurance market. It then describes the proposed legislation and the reaction of the health insurance industry. Chapter Three describes the structure of the HIAA analysis. It then presents a detailed discussion of the sources for HIAA's figures and the corresponding figures used in our estimates. The end of that chapter presents a range of estimates based on combinations of assumptions. Chapter Four discusses the interaction of these estimates of the increase in the average claim costs per individual insurance policy with state insurance regulations. Chapter Five summarizes the results of the analysis. The appendix provides considerable detail about the underlying data sources, how the data were used, and more details from our new tabulations.

Chapter Two

POLICY BACKGROUND

This chapter describes the policy context of the analysis presented in Chapter Three. It begins by describing the generic problem with the health insurance market and previous policy responses. It then describes the proposed legislation and responses to it.

THE MARKET FOR INSURANCE

Unlike the life insurance market, the health insurance market in the United States operates year by year. Having health insurance in one year currently provides little guarantee of the availability of coverage or its price in future years. To some extent, this problem is ameliorated by the fact that health insurance is usually sold to groups. Inasmuch as the groups are large, expensive illnesses to individual group members do not have large effects on the availability or price of insurance. In addition, state regulation of health insurance guarantees some form of insurance availability and/or price regulation.

Many people, including many of those working for small employers or changing jobs, are protected neither by group sale nor by current state insurance regulation. Given the current structure of the market, individuals/firms cannot buy protection against unexpected and unpredictable increases in expected health care claims (and thus in health insurance premiums). Instead, under the current system, when the current insurance year ends (for small groups) or when a job change occurs (for individuals), the insurance company can raise insurance rates to cover the expected cost of insurance claims for the coming year. Thus, an in-principle "insurable" risk—expenditures that are not predictable when the insurance was originally purchased and that can be averaged out over many policies—is not insurable under current institutional arrangements.[1] Instead, health insurance purchased today covers the unpredictable part of health care this year; but not the changes in our best guess about health care costs in future years.

This aspect of the operation of the health insurance market has produced several problems. First, for some individuals, coverage is simply not available (insurers refuse to sell them insurance), or is available only at very high cost. Second, some individuals are "locked" into their jobs by the fear (often real) that if they leave their job they will be ineligible for health insurance—either forever or for some waiting period—or that their "preexisting conditions" ("preexisting" with respect to the new job, even if not with respect to the old job) will not be covered—either forever or for some waiting period.[2]

In the mid-1980s several states and then the federal government (as part of the Consolidated Omnibus Budget Reconciliation Act of 1986, hereafter simply COBRA) enacted legislation to partially ameliorate this situation. The federal legislation gives terminating employees the right to buy health insurance at 102 percent of the group rate for up to 18 months after leaving a job. The legislation applies both to workers who are fired and to those who quit. The major exceptions were employees terminated for gross malfeasance and employees at firms with fewer than 20 employees. The legislation appears to have had a moderate effect on health insurance coverage of job leavers.[3]

THE HEALTH INSURANCE REFORM ACT OF 1995

The proposed Health Insurance Reform Act of 1995 would address other aspects of this situation. It would limit the length of preexisting conditions clauses, make it illegal to deny coverage to any em-

---

[1] See Cochrane (1995) for a more complete development of this idea about the relationship between insurability and the current structure of health insurance contracts.

[2] On "job lock," see Madrian (1994) and Holtz-Eakin (1994).

[3] On the effects of COBRA on levels of health insurance coverage, see Klerman and Rahman (1992) and Gruber and Madrian (1994, 1995). The more general literature on COBRA also includes Flynn (1992, 1994) and Long and Marquis (1992).

ployer with two or more employees, guarantee the renewability of health insurance coverage, make it easier for employers and individuals to form private voluntary coalitions to purchase health insurance, and extend COBRA protections to disabled workers and newborns.

The legislation, however, has essentially no provisions about the pricing of the guaranteed health insurance package. Thus, while insurers must offer health insurance, they can price it prohibitively high without violating the provisions of the law. The insurance rate regulations of some states (also called "rate bands") would prohibit such behavior in those states.[4] We return to the effect of state insurance regulations in Chapter Four.

Most of the bill has received broad support. The major exception is a "conversion coverage" provision. This provision is intended to help individuals who leave a job maintain health insurance. It requires that workers who have been continuously covered by an employer-sponsored group health insurance plan for 18 months, but who cannot now purchase any group health insurance (through a current employer, through a spouse, or through a previous employer via COBRA), be allowed to convert their group coverage into individual coverage.

This conversion provision of the bill has been opposed by the HIAA. In a statement titled *The Cost of Ending "Job Lock" or How Much Would Health Insurance Costs Go Up If "Portability" of Health Insurance Were Guaranteed? Preliminary Estimates—July 26, 1995,* HIAA concludes:[5]

---

[4]For more discussion of the interaction of state insurance regulation and the proposed legislation, see American Academy of Actuaries (1996a, b) and Hustead (1996). See also the "Caveat" to HIAA's press release on the proposed legislation (HIAA, 1995) and Gradison (1996).

[5]As of March 1996, this statement remained HIAA's position on this issue. Furthermore, HIAA continues to stand behind the analysis reported there. See for example the statement quoted in the name of Bill Gradison (HIAA's president) that

the effect of allowing people to purchase the individual coverage "would be to raise premiums for people who already have individual coverage—by anywhere from 10 to up to 30 percent" (Clymer, 1996).

Clymer's story continues stating that

Initially, the average premium for people insured through the individual market is likely to increase by between 10% and 19%, with a most likely estimate of 15%. In the longer run, increases of 15% to 31% are likely, with a most likely estimate of 22%. If spread equally across all individual policyholders, increases of this magnitude are likely to cause more than two-thirds of a million relatively healthy policy holders to drop coverage.

This HIAA analysis and these cost estimates have been widely quoted in the general press.[6] In particular, the HIAA opposition to the conversion provision has been cited as the cause of a hold on the legislation in the Senate.[7]

More recently, in response to analyses of the bill by the American Academy of Actuaries (AAA, 1996b) and Hay-Huggins (Hustead, 1996), HIAA released an "alternative" analysis (Gradison, 1996; Wildsmith, 1996); we will refer to the original HIAA estimates as "HIAA I" and the more recent HIAA estimates as "HIAA II". HIAA explains its reasons for releasing an alternative estimate as follows:

In the interests of defusing unproductive disputes over non-critical assumptions, and to clarify the differences of true significance, this paper recasts the original HIAA cost estimates using those assumptions from the American Academy of Actuaries estimate that we consider non-critical. The purpose is not to suggest that the AAA assumptions are superior to those originally used by HIAA, but merely to focus discussion on the most important differences in assumptions (Gradison, 1996).

The next chapter analyzes both of the HIAA estimates and presents new estimates based on better underlying figures.

Richard Coorsh, a spokesman for the insurance association, . . . said that his organization was seeking to explain to the actuaries why it believed the higher cost estimates.

[6]See for example Gray (1996), Jouzaitis (1996), and Chen (1996).

[7]See for example Gray (1996), Dewar (1996), and the other newspaper articles cited in the previous two footnotes.

Chapter Three

THE HIAA METHODOLOGY: ORIGINAL AND RAND ESTIMATES

We begin this chapter by describing the HIAA methodology, its basic assumptions, and the required figures to perform the implied calculations. We then provide a discussion of the sources for the figures used in the two HIAA analyses and the revised figures. The appendix provides additional information on HIAA's data sources, as well as the data sources themselves, how they are used, and the results underlying our revised figures.

THE HEALTH INSURANCE MARKET

To understand the HIAA methodology, it is useful to define three groups of people:

1. Those with conventional employer-sponsored health insurance in firms with 20 or more employees. Under COBRA, individuals leaving such employers (each worker and his or her dependents) have the right to purchase continuation coverage when the employee separates from the employer. Under that continuation coverage, each could continue to participate in the previous employer's group health insurance plan. He or she would pay a premium of up to 102 percent of the employer's cost for the insurance and this continuation coverage is limited to 18 months.

2. Those with conventional employer-sponsored health insurance in firms with less than 20 employees. COBRA does not guarantee them the right to any continuation coverage when they leave the firm.

3. Those currently—in the absence of the proposed legislation—
purchasing insurance in the individual health insurance market.
We will refer to them as the "current participants in the individual
health insurance market" and sometimes with an "IND" subscript.

The effects of the proposed federal legislation would vary for these
different groups, and the proposed legislation's impact is affected by
the group's relative size in the absence of the legislation.

To be guaranteed the right to the proposed legislation's conversion
insurance, the individual must have been continuously enrolled in a
group health insurance plan for 18 months and not be eligible for any
other group health insurance (through a current employer, through a
spouse, or through COBRA). For individuals covered by firms with 20
or more employees, such eligibility would begin at the end of the 18
months of COBRA coverage. For individuals covered by firms with
fewer than 20 employees, such eligibility would begin when they
leave the job, but only if they have been continuously covered by
group health insurance for 18 months (on this job or on a previous
job). We refer to these people as "new participants in the individual
health insurance market" (and sometimes with a "K-K" subscript,
which refers to S. 1028 by Senators Kassebaum and Kennedy).

THE HIAA ANALYSES

The HIAA methodology computes the average increase in premiums
in the individual health insurance market.[1] The basic algebra is as

---

[1]See the HIAA quote from HIAA, 1996, in Chapter Two, which carefully states "If
spread equally across all individual policy holders. . . ." That condition is expanded in
a following "Caveat":

> The premium rating rules imposed by states will determine how the additional costs of
> "group-to-individual" portability are spread across the individual market. This
> distribution, in turn, will have a direct impact on the affordability of coverage and thus
> on the number and type of purchasers and on the aggregate cost of the portability re-
> quirement.

> Since it is not known how the various states would choose to regulate premiums for
> portability coverage, there is a natural limit to the accuracy of any cost estimates.
> Therefore, this paper assumes that states regulation will make the coverage relatively
> affordable (relative to standard coverage in the individual market) and estimates the
> aggregate cost increases to the individual insurance market. The estimates are not in-
> tended to predict how states would regulate rates to spread the additional costs across

follows. Denote average claims without the proposed legislation (i.e., claims of those currently in the individual insurance market—"old average claims) as AC_{IND}. Denote average claims among those entering the individual insurance market as a result of the proposed legislation as $AC_{K\text{-}K}$. Then average claims with the proposed legislation ("New Average Claims") will be a weighted average of the average claims of those currently purchasing individual insurance and the new entrants:[2]

$$\text{New Average Claims} = \frac{\left(N_{IND} \times AC_{IND}\right) + \left(N_{K-K} \times AC_{K-K}\right)}{N_{IND} + N_{K-K}}. \tag{1}$$

The weights are given by the relative size of the two groups, i.e., the number of people currently buying individual health insurance and

---

the market, however, they do assume that liability for any increases is borne only by purchasers of individual policies.

[2]We note that this analysis framework assumes no price effect. This is true in two senses. First, inasmuch as the new entrants face higher premiums, there may be fewer of them than is implied by the calculation of $N_{K\text{-}K}$ in Eq. 1. This will imply that our estimated effects of the proposed legislation are too low. Second, inasmuch as the premiums of those currently purchasing health insurance rise because of the proposed legislation, fewer of the buyers will purchase it. This will imply that our estimated effects of the proposed legislation are too high.

HIAA includes some estimates of the second effect in a secondary analysis. This effect is, however, not included in their statements about price effects. We ignore it here. We note below that our analysis suggests that premiums for those currently purchasing health insurance will not rise by very much (a few percentage points at most). Given the literature on the price elasticity of health insurance purchase (e.g., Marquis and Long, 1995), which suggests that the elasticities are well below 1, the effects on the calculations in the body of the report will be trivial.

However, the body of the report extrapolates likely take-up rates for the conversion coverage based on COBRA continuation coverage (for the sub-COBRA population) and universal take-up rates by assumption (for the COBRA population). Because of higher loading costs in the individual market, conversion coverage is likely to be much more expensive than COBRA continuation coverage. In that case, these estimated take-up rates are probably too high, and then our final estimated effects of the legislation are also too large.

Given that our best estimates imply small changes in the price of individual insurance, the total effect of the considerations raised in this footnote is likely to be small (even relative to our small estimates). Furthermore, the effects of the previous paragraph are likely to dominate. Thus, these considerations are another reason why our final estimates are too large.

the number of additional people who would buy because of the proposed legislation (N_{IND} and N_{K-K}, respectively).

We can then compute average claims in the individual insurance market with the proposed legislation relative to average claims without the proposed legislation as:

$$\text{Relative Average Claims} = \frac{\text{New Average Claims}}{\text{Old Average Claims}}$$

$$= \frac{N_{IND} + \left(N_{K-K} \times \left(AC_{K-K}/AC_{IND}\right)\right)}{N_{IND} + N_{K-K}}. \tag{2}$$

Defining the relative cost of the new buyers to the current buyers as:

$$RC_{K-K} = \frac{AC_{K-K}}{AC_{IND}}, \tag{3}$$

we arrive at the basic relation used in the analysis below:

$$\text{Relative Average Claims} = \frac{\text{New Average Claims}}{\text{Old Average Claims}}$$

$$= \frac{N_{IND} + \left(N_{K-K} \times RC_{K-K}\right)}{N_{IND} + N_{K-K}}. \tag{4}$$

Some HIAA statements use these estimates of the increase in the *average claims cost* (or in the average premium) in the individual insurance market to estimate the increase in the premiums of *those currently purchasing individual health insurance* (see Gradison's statement of February 1996, quoted in footnote 5 in Chapter Two; and Gradison, 1996). Doing so requires an assumption that insurance companies will charge the same premium for these continuation policies as for the current individual insurance policies. We return to this use of the estimates in the next chapter.

To estimate the effect on average premiums in the individual health insurance market (regardless of how insurance companies price the two types of policies), we need three figures: RC_{K-K}, N_{IND}, and N_{K-K}. HIAA's methodology for the estimation of N_{K-K} and the total effect

Table 1

Premium Effects: Original HIAA Estimates and RAND Estimates

	HIAA		HIAA-RAND		RAND-Best	
	COBRA	Sub-COBRA	COBRA	Sub-COBRA	COBRA	Sub-COBRA
Covered lives (in millions)	120.0	30.0	124.5	13.2	124.5	13.2
Percentage leaving job (per year)	12.0%	20.0%	16.6%	24.6%	16.6%	24.6%
Percentage of job leavers eligible for the program	4.0%	100.0%	0.8%	88.3%	0.8%	88.3%
Insured years per eligible person	2.00	0.30	2.00	0.11	2.00	0.11
Total insured years (in millions)	1.15	1.80	0.31	0.32	0.31	0.32
Ratio of claims costs of new policies to those of current policies	200%	200%	200%	200%	150%	150%
Current insured years (in millions)	10.4		10.4		13.1	
Increase in average premium	22.1%		5.7%		2.3%	

NOTE: HIAA data are computed from HIAA, 1995.

(along with the specific HIAA estimate and our RAND estimate) is summarized in Table 1.

This table does not appear in the HIAA report. We use it because it provides a useful framework for understanding the HIAA estimates and the methodology for our estimates. The table consists of three pairs of columns. The first pair of columns (from the left; labeled "HIAA") presents the original HIAA analysis ("HIAA I") in terms of this framework. The number on the final line, 22.1 percent, is exactly the original HIAA estimate ("HIAA I") of the "most likely" "long-run" average premium increase in the individual insurance market as a result of the proposed legislation. The second pair of columns substitutes the newly computed figures ("HIAA-RAND") but otherwise maintains the "HIAA I" assumptions. The third pair of columns presents our preferred estimate ("RAND-Best"). It alters some of the HIAA assumptions to values that, in our opinion, more closely correspond to the likely outcome of the proposed legislation.

The HIAA methodology computes the number of new participants in the individual market N_{K-K} as the sum of

- new participants from the COBRA market (the left column of each panel, individuals with insurance from firms with 20 or more employees) and

- new participants from the sub-COBRA market (the right column of each panel, individuals with insurance from firms with fewer than 20 employees).

Within each column, the number of new participants (the fifth row, labeled "total insured years") is computed as the product of the first four rows. To have conversion coverage at a point in time, a covered life at a point in time (the first row) must leave his or her job (the second row) and be eligible for the program (the third row). The fourth row gives the number of insured years per eligible individual (i.e., the product of the first three rows). In principle, computation of the first two rows is straightforward. Estimating the third and fourth rows requires additional assumptions that we discuss in detail below.

The last four rows compute the estimate of the effect on average premiums in the individual health insurance market. The fifth row gives the number of new participants, N_{K-K}, for each sector (computed as the product of the first four rows). The sixth row gives the assumed value for relative claim costs, RC_{K-K}. The seventh row gives the number of individuals in the individual market, N_{IND}. The eighth row gives the implied estimate of the increase in average claim costs per insured life.

DISCUSSION OF TABLE ENTRIES

In this section, we discuss in turn each of the rows of Table 1. For each row, we begin by describing the sources for the HIAA estimates (HIAA I and HIAA II) and where appropriate (i.e., for rows three and four) explaining the logic behind estimating each row in a particular way. We then briefly discuss our data and methods (used in RAND-HIAA I, RAND-HIAA II, RAND-Best I, and RAND-Best II) and compare their suitability and quality to those used by HIAA. The appendix discusses in more detail the data and how they were analyzed. It also and presents more complete results.

Population Estimates

We begin by considering the size of the populations: How many people are covered by group health insurance policies from an employer with 20 or more employees (and thus are eligible for COBRA continuation coverage)? How many people are covered by group health insurance policies from an employer with fewer than 20 employees (and are thus not eligible for COBRA continuation coverage)? And, How many people are currently covered by individual health insurance policies?

The basic data for most of the HIAA population estimates and our reestimates are derived from the March Demographic Supplement to the Current Population Survey (hereafter simply CPS), a large nationally representative annual survey conducted by the U.S. Bureau of the Census. These questions nominally refer to the previous calendar year. Most analysts interpret responses as referring to status as of the interview date (EBRI, 1996).

The original HIAA analysis ("HIAA I") was based on the 1994 CPS. Since HIAA's original analysis, the 1995 CPS data have been released. These data are preferred, not only because they are more recent, but also because they are based on a revised and more detailed set of health insurance questions that were specifically designed to improve the quality of the data (EBRI, 1996). The questions on which these data are based appear to have had the twin effects of increasing the number of people reporting employer-based coverage and lowering the number of people reporting individual coverage. In addition, the new questions appear to have substantially improved the reporting of children's health insurance.

HIAA I estimates the size of the COBRA and sub-COBRA markets at 120 million and 30 million respectively. As we discuss in detail in the Technical Appendix, these figures are apparently derived based on the 1994 data and the assumption that everyone with employer-based coverage who is not known to be in a large firm is in a small firm. HIAA II uses the American Academy of Actuaries' (AAA) estimates of 127.5 million and 18.4 million, respectively, based on AAA (1996b) analysis of the 1995 CPS data.

Based on the 1995 CPS data, our preferred figures are 124.5 million and 13.2 million, respectively. Consistent with the changes between the 1994 and 1995 CPS, relative to the HIAA I estimates, these figures are slightly higher for the COBRA market and much lower for the sub-COBRA market.

These alternative figures are based on the 1995 data, an allocation of those with unknown firm size (i.e., those who are reported as "nonworkers" or those working in firms with 10–24 employees), and the exclusion of the self-employed. The exclusion of the self-employed explains most of the difference between our figure and the AAA figure (the rest appears to be because of the allocation of the nonworkers; see the appendix). We exclude the self-employed because many of them are in fact purchasing individual insurance (and are thus ineligible for the proposed legislation's guarantees). Those among the self-employed who are purchasing group coverage have much smaller turnover rates than those implied by our calculations for employees by firm size (see the next chapter) or by the employee turnover rates used by HIAA.

The HIAA methodology also requires an estimate of the number of those currently covered by individual health insurance. It is the base to which the new conversion policies will be added. For this figure, HIAA uses its own estimate of the size of the individual insurance market, 10.4 million covered lives. This estimate is derived from insurance industry sources on the number of covered lives. It is based on a narrow definition of the "individual insurance market" as including only policies currently sold and regulated as "individual insurance."

Our HIAA-RAND estimates maintain this narrow concept of the individual insurance market and the HIAA estimate. Our RAND-Best estimate adopts the broader concept of the individual insurance market proposed by the AAA (1996b). That broader concept includes insurance policies priced on an individual basis (e.g., discretionary group trusts, association group coverage, and list-based health insurance provided to small firms). HIAA (Wildsmith, 1996) has criticized this concept noting that

> those other arrangements are not regulated as part of the individual health insurance market. Statutes generally apply to things as they are legally defined. Absent statutory changes at the state level, it seems inappropriate to include these miscellaneous forms of coverage in the individual market.

Because this position has some validity, we use the HIAA estimate in the HIAA-RAND estimate. However, as we discuss in detail in the next chapter, if state regulations do not change (as is implied by the quote from Wildsmith, 1996), in all but five states the proposed federal legislation will have no effect. The HIAA analysis would be broadly applicable only if many more states move to regulate individual health insurance premiums. HIAA's efforts (among others) have made/will make states well aware of the issue of what to consider an individual policy. For exactly these reasons, when (and if) states adopt rate regulation in response to the proposed federal legislation, they are likely to use a broad conceptualization of the individual market.

Using this broader concept and the AAA (1996b) allocation of the nonemployer-based private insurance group, we conservatively estimate the size of this market as 80 percent of the 1995 CPS figure for all individuals who report private (nongovernment) insurance, but not through an employer. Applying this allocation to the 1995 CPS figure yields the RAND-Best estimate of 13.1 million covered lives in the (broadly defined) individual health insurance market.[3]

Percentage Leaving a Job

To be eligible for the conversion coverage, an employee must first leave his or her job. HIAA I assumes annual turnover rates of 12 percent in the COBRA-insurance market and 20 percent in the sub-COBRA-insurance market. Following AAA, HIAA II assumes a 12 percent turnover rate in both markets.

Our estimates are based on new tabulations from the SIPP. These data imply *higher* annual job-leaving rates than either HIAA I or AAA/HIAA II, 16.6 and 24.6, respectively. They thus imply larger effects of the proposed legislation on the individual insurance market.

---

[3]This figure is computed as 80 percent of the 1995 CPS figure of 16.4 million. The assumption that 80 percent of the "other private" is truly individual coverage is the lower end of the range given by the American Academy of Actuaries (AAA, 1996b). The upper end of the range is 90 percent. Our choice of the lower end of the range implies that our final estimates of the effect of the proposed legislation are too large.

Percentage Program Eligible

Not all job leavers are eligible for the program, and program eligibility computations are quite different for the two groups. For the COBRA-coverage population, program eligibility requires both COBRA-coverage take-up and continued COBRA coverage for the full 18 months (until they "exhaust" COBRA coverage). HIAA I estimates the COBRA-coverage take-up rate at 20 percent and that 20 percent of all people who take up COBRA coverage exhaust it (the HIAA I figure in the table is computed as $0.2 \times 0.2 = 0.04$). Following AAA, HIAA II estimates the COBRA-coverage take-up rate at 20 percent and that 25 percent of those taking up COBRA coverage exhaust it (the HIAA II figure is computed as $0.2 \times 0.25 = 0.05$).

The COBRA-coverage take-up rate figures are based on a survey of employers' experiences as reported in Spencer & Associates (1991). As we discuss in the appendix, the Spencer data overrepresent large firms and because of this and other issues about the selectivity of firms responding to such surveys, these estimates are likely to be higher than the true take-up rates.

HIAA's COBRA-coverage exhaustion figure of 20 percent is apparently based on unpublished tabulations of the time not employed and health insurance status (currently and on the previous job) of the currently unemployed. These tabulations were compiled by Klerman and Rahman for HIAA in the early 1990s. Related tabulations were published in Klerman and Rahman (1992). The tabulations were based on the 1984, 1985, and 1986 panels of the SIPP. Since the interviews for those panels did not distinguish health insurance provided by a current employer from health insurance provided by a previous employer, those tabulations cannot be used to explore COBRA coverage (some of which is used after the individual is reemployed). Thus, the applicability of those tabulations to the percentage of COBRA-coverage participants who exhaust COBRA coverage is not clear.

Our revised figures are based on new tabulations from the SIPP. While other analyses (HIAA, 1995, 1996; AAA, 1996b) have used a two-step computation, we believe that it is easier to use a one-step procedure, given data issues related to the SIPP (which we discuss in detail below). Instead of estimating separately the COBRA-coverage take-up rate and then the average duration on COBRA coverage or the exhaustion rate among those who take up, we attempt to directly estimate the number of months on COBRA coverage per job leaver (i.e., among all job leavers, whether or not they ever use COBRA coverage) and the percentage of all job leavers who exhaust COBRA coverage.

The exact data and analysis is described in detail in the appendix. The basic idea is a statistical generalization of following a group of COBRA-eligible covered lives forward from job leaving. We could then estimate the proportion exhausting COBRA coverage as the fraction of all job leavers who report health insurance from a previous employer in the 18th month after job leaving, but not in the 19th month. Our procedure yields a figure of 0.8 percent; only eight covered lives per thousand job leavers actually exhaust COBRA coverage.

This RAND estimate deliberately errs on the side of being *too high* (making our estimates of the effects of the proposed legislation on the individual insurance market too large). Because of data limitations, it is computed under the assumption that all workers who report health insurance coverage through a previous employer were COBRA-coverage eligible and that everyone who stops being covered by a previous employer in months 17, 18, 19, or 20 has exhausted COBRA coverage. Both of these assumptions are conservative. It appears that a considerable number of individuals from small firms (fewer than 25 employees) also report health insurance coverage through a previous employer. In addition, some of the people who end "previous-employer" coverage during months 17, 18, 19, and 20 do so, not because they have exhausted COBRA coverage, but because they have acquired some other source of coverage (Medicare, Medicaid, another employer, a spouse's employer, etc.).

Both HIAA analyses assume that everyone in the sub-COBRA-insurance market would be eligible for the conversion option. This appears to be an overestimate. The proposed legislation requires 18 continuous months of group health insurance coverage for an individual to be eligible for conversion. For individuals in the COBRA-insurance market, these 18 months could all be acquired through COBRA insurance. For individuals in the sub-COBRA-insurance market, these 18 months must be acquired before leaving the job.

Based on the SIPP, we estimate that 77 percent of those currently employed in a sub-COBRA-coverage firm have job tenure of more than 18 months. All of them would be eligible for conversion. The other 23 percent would not be eligible for conversion coverage based solely on insurance at the current job. Some of them will have been continuously insured (e.g., they came directly to this job from a job from which they had had health insurance for 18 months). From the SIPP, we are unable to estimate how common this is. We have arbitrarily assumed that half of the 23 percent with job tenure of under 18 months gain eligibility in this way (through a previous job). Thus, we estimate that 88 percent of those leaving sub-COBRA-coverage jobs will be eligible for the conversion coverage. The estimate that half of those without sufficient job tenure nevertheless had 18 continuous months of health insurance is likely to be too high, and thus the final estimates of the effect of the proposed legislation are too high.

Insured Years Per Program-Eligible Person

Given that we know how many covered lives there are, what share of them leave a job in a year, and what share of them would be eligible for conversion coverage, we need to know the number of years covered by the conversion policy per program-eligible individual. Again, the results differ by market. We maintain the HIAA assumption that all of those exhausting COBRA coverage would use conversion coverage. We also maintain the HIAA assumptions of the average length of time that those exhausting COBRA coverage would buy conversion coverage: two years in HIAA I and three years in HIAA II.

For the sub-COBRA-insurance market, HIAA I assumed that 20 percent of those leaving sub-COBRA-coverage jobs would take the conversion coverage and that they would stay on conversion coverage an average of 18 months (1.5 years). The figure in Table 1 for years of conversion coverage per eligible individual is $0.20 \times 1.5 = 0.30$ (i.e., the percentage of those ever using continuation coverage times the percentage of those ever using conversion coverage who exhaust it).

HIAA II follows the AAA figure for the average duration of conversion coverage—2.25 years.[4]

Our estimate of the average time per eligible person follows the HIAA I assumption that when offered conversion coverage, individuals in the sub-COBRA-insurance market will use it the way individuals in the COBRA-insurance market use COBRA insurance. Our estimate of the way individuals in the COBRA-insurance market use COBRA insurance is based on our tabulations from the SIPP. Unlike HIAA, which computes the probability of ever using continuation coverage (COBRA insurance) and then the average duration of people who ever use coverage, we use SIPP data since it is more appropriate to tabulate the average number of years of continuation coverage per each job leaver (see the appendix for our exact methods and the appropriate caveats).

To this estimate from SIPP of years on COBRA insurance per eligible job leaver, we add the appropriate HIAA estimate of the average duration of conversion coverage among those eligible for COBRA coverage who exhaust the COBRA coverage—two years in HIAA I/SIPP I and three years in HIAA II/SIPP II (based on AAA, 1996b). From our SIPP tabulations plus the assumed time after COBRA-coverage exhaustion (among those who exhaust COBRA coverage), we estimate time using conversion coverage per job leaver at about a month (0.118 years and 0.125 years for SIPP I and SIPP II, respectively).

For two reasons, this estimate is likely to be too high (and therefore our estimates of the effect on the individual health insurance market too high). First, this estimate assumes that all of the observed previous-employer coverage is from the COBRA-insurance market. In fact, some of the current previous-employer coverage is probably from the sub-COBRA-insurance market. If so, we have overestimated the amount of COBRA coverage. In addition, inasmuch as some individuals in the sub-COBRA-insurance market already get continuation coverage (even though it is not required by statute, i.e.,

---

[4]It should be noted that HIAA II does not accept the AAA assumption that the take-up rate in the sub-COBRA market will be "6% to 10%" (AAA, 1996b, p. A-2, note 9). Doing so would cut the HIAA estimate by nearly 3 percentage points. AAA also notes that the percentage would be even lower if, as seems likely, conversion policy premiums are much higher than standard individual insurance premiums.

by COBRA), we should net out this coverage from the total effect on the individual market. Our estimates do not take such considerations into account and are thus likely to be too large.

Second, COBRA insurance is available at group rates. The conversion coverage will be at the higher individual rates (because of higher loading factors in the individual market). These higher rates are likely to discourage some people (who would have participated at COBRA-insurance rates) from participating. We have ignored both of these reasons.

Our estimates differ considerably from those in the published literature (e.g., Flynn, 1992). As we discuss in the appendix, the results in the published literature are based on surveys of employers, or on records of intermediaries that process COBRA-insurance plans. Neither of these sources is nationally representative. Large firms are heavily overrepresented. We suspect that firm size and the types of firms using intermediaries to respond to surveys cause an overestimate of COBRA-insurance take-up rates and COBRA-insurance durations. However, if in the SIPP individuals report COBRA coverage as private insurance not through an employer (as opposed to private insurance through a previous employer), then the SIPP-based estimates will be too low. As we discuss in the appendix, the nature of COBRA coverage suggests that this misreporting is unlikely to be large.

Relative Claims Cost

The final figure for the HIAA methodology is the claim costs of conversion coverage relative to those currently buying individual insurance, RC_{K-K}. The required figures are a standard actuarial computation of expected claim costs.

The HIAA I estimate assumes that the relative claims cost of the conversion policies will be twice that of current individual insurance policies. They explain this figure as "Intermediate between estimates of COBRA experience and individual high risk pool experience" (HIAA, 1995). The COBRA-insurance experience is that claims are about 150 percent of the relevant *group claim cost*. Since the average COBRA-insurance enrollee is older than the average group insured individual (see Flynn, 1992), not all of this difference is a pure morbidity effect. Since most current states allow premiums to vary with age (see the next chapter), even this estimate of 150 percent is higher than the relevant concept.

Furthermore, this 150 percent figure refers to the COBRA-insurance period. Presumably, HIAA uses a higher figure (200 percent) because people who exhaust COBRA coverage are presumably sicker than those who have relatively short COBRA-coverage experiences. Note, however, that the COBRA-coverage cost estimate of 150 percent is likely to mix three groups of people. The first is a group of those of normal risk who want to maintain coverage. The second is a group of people who know they have upcoming expenses (e.g., planned surgery, pregnancy, etc.). They will have high costs in the months immediately after take-up but, over the longer term, their claim costs will be closer to those of normal risk. Finally, there will be a group of people with chronically higher costs. They are likely to exhaust COBRA coverage and to take up the conversion coverage. These are the people who might push up the cost of continuation coverage. As we discuss in detail in the next chapter, in many states these people are likely to be shifted to the high-risk pool (almost all states have such a pool, and it is intended to subsidize the insurance of people with chronically high costs).

The RAND-Best estimate uses a 150 percent relative claim cost estimate in both markets (rather than the HIAA I estimate of 200 percent). Inasmuch as take-up of continuation coverage in the sub-COBRA-insurance market is like take-up in the current COBRA-insurance market (as HIAA assumes), it seems reasonable to assume that the relative costs of those in the sub-COBRA-insurance market will be similar to current COBRA-insurance costs. In the COBRA-insurance market after exhaustion, it seems more plausible to assume that the 150 percent figure is driven up by those who expect expensive procedures shortly after take-up, so that the 150 percent figure would also be a good estimate of the relative cost of those with chronically higher costs. Because this is a matter of judgment, we report both the RAND-Best estimate based on this lower value, and the RAND-HIAA estimate based on the original HIAA assumption of 200 percent.

COMPARING THE HIAA ESTIMATES AND THE RAND ESTIMATES

Table 1 (on page 13) presents three estimates of the increase in average costs per individual insurance policy. The original HIAA estimate (HIAA I) was an increase of 22.1 percent. Using the same methodology, but our better figures, our corresponding RAND estimate (HIAA-RAND) is an increase of 5.7 percent.

Our preferred estimate, however, (RAND-Best) alters two of the HIAA assumptions. It uses the broader concept of the size of the individual market over which claims will be pooled (13.1 million versus 10.4 million), and it uses the COBRA-insurance relative claims cost for conversion coverage in both sectors (150 percent versus 200 percent). This estimate is an increase of 2.3 percent.

In both of its analyses, HIAA also explored the sensitivity of its estimates to alternative values for the cost of claims in both the COBRA-insurance and sub-COBRA-insurance sectors. Tables 2 and 3 report the results of those sensitivity analyses for all three assumptions (HIAA, HIAA-RAND, and RAND-Best). Table 2 maintains the HIAA I assumptions (for length of time after COBRA-insurance exhaustion). Table 3 maintains the HIAA II assumptions.

The base case (the first row) maintains the HIAA assumption that the claims under conversion policies will be twice those under existing individual policies. The first alternative (the second row) corresponds to the RAND-Best assumption that all conversion policies will have claims similar to the COBRA-insurance rate (150 percent of the current individual rate). The second alternative considers the possibility that claims for those in the sub-COBRA-insurance market will be similar to claims in the current COBRA-insurance market, approximately one and a half times those in the current individual market, but maintains the assumption that claims in the COBRA-insurance market after COBRA-insurance exhaustion will be twice those in the individual market. The third and fourth alternative (the fourth and fifth rows) consider increasing the average claims cost in the COBRA-insurance market under the assumption that only people with very high claims costs (sicker or older) would buy conversion coverage after the full 18 months of COBRA coverage. HIAA I uses a high estimate of three times individual claims costs. That 300 percent figure also appears in the equation for the higher estimate in HIAA II. The text in HIAA II, however, reads "250%" and the final number is correct for two and a half times the cost of individual claims (but not for three times the cost of individual claims). We present the full range of estimates for completeness.

While the HIAA estimates reach 32.4 percent (or 40.8 percent in the number they do not report), the highest RAND-Best estimate is only 7.5 percent (9.2 percent). As is discussed below, even these numbers are too high.

Finally, it should be noted that even this HIAA-RAND estimate of 5.7 and this RAND-Best estimate of 2.3 percent are conservative. At several places, the figures were deliberately computed using the more conservative estimate (implying larger effect of the law) from among a range or in interpreting our tabulations. In particular, our analysis

Table 2

**Sensitivity of Estimates to Relative Cost (RC) Assumptions,
Given HIAA I Assumptions
(in percentage)**

Assumptions	HIAA I	HIAA-RAND	RAND-Best
Basic HIAA I assumption (also used in HIAA-RAND)[a]	*22.1*	5.7	4.6
RAND-Best assumption[b]	11.1	2.9	2.3
Lower value in the HIAA I and HIAA II sensitivity analysis[c]	*15.4*	4.3	3.4
Upper value in the HIAA I sensitivity analysis[d]	*30.7*	8.5	6.9
Upper value in the HIAA II sensitivity analysis[e]	26.4	7.1	5.7

NOTE: Entries in italics appear in HIAA (1995).

[a]RC-COBRA = 200 percent, RC-sub-COBRA = 200 percent.

[b]RC-COBRA = 150 percent, RC-sub-COBRA = 150 percent.

[c]RC-COBRA = 200 percent, RC-sub-COBRA = 150 percent.

[d]RC-COBRA = 300 percent, RC-sub-COBRA = 200 percent.

[e]RC-COBRA = 250 percent, RC-sub-COBRA = 200 percent.

Table 3

Sensitivity of Estimates to Relative Cost (RC) Assumptions, Given HIAA II Assumptions
(in percentage)

Assumptions	HIAA II	HIAA-RAND	RAND-Best
Basic HIAA I assumption (also used in HIAA-RAND)[a]	_24.0_	7.2	5.8
RAND-Best assumption[b]	12.0	3.6	2.9
Lower value in the HIAA I and HIAA II sensitivity analysis[c]	_20.4_	5.7	4.6
Upper value in the HIAA I sensitivity analysis[d]	40.8	11.4	9.2
Upper value in the HIAA II sensitivity analysis[e]	_32.4_	9.3	7.5

NOTE: Entries in italics appear in HIAA (1996).

[a]RC-COBRA = 200 percent, RC-sub-COBRA = 200 percent.

[b]RC-COBRA = 150 percent, RC-sub-COBRA = 150 percent.

[c]RC-COBRA = 200 percent, RC-sub-COBRA = 150 percent.

[d]RC-COBRA = 300 percent, RC-sub-COBRA = 200 percent.

[e]RC-COBRA = 250 percent, RC-sub-COBRA = 200 percent.

assumes that all of the observed insurance through a previous employer is from COBRA-insurance-eligible individuals. Limited tabulations suggest that, in fact, there is considerable coverage from a previous employer even among individuals in the sub-COBRA-insurance market (the HIAA methodology essentially implies that no such coverage occurs). If so, our figures for COBRA-insurance take-up rates are too high and our figures for COBRA-coverage durations are too long. For similar reasons, the number of new entrants to the individual insurance market should be computed netting out those with coverage from a previous employer. Our figures do not do so.

In addition, we have not considered the effect of the high cost of health insurance in the individual market (relative to the COBRA-insurance market). Following HIAA, we have assumed that, despite being faced with the higher individual market premiums, individuals will purchase conversion coverage at the same rate that individuals in the COBRA-insurance market purchase COBRA coverage. Due to larger loading factors, premiums in the individual market are much higher than in the large group market (on which COBRA-insurance premiums are based). Similarly, COBRA-insurance premiums are based on the health insurance premium across all employees. Inasmuch as individuals insured under COBRA tend to be older than the average employee (see Flynn, 1992), their premiums in the individual market—where premiums vary with age—will be even higher. Thus, for several reasons, the revised HIAA-methodology-based estimates of the effect of the proposed federal legislation on average premiums in the individual insurance market presented in this chapter should be considered an upper bound; the true estimate is probably lower.

Chapter Four

THE EFFECTS OF STATE REGULATION

The previous chapter presented the HIAA methodology and new and improved estimates of the underlying figures. As HIAA notes (see the "Caveat" in footnote 1 in Chapter Three), its methodology estimates the *increase in the average individual health insurance premium* due to the proposed legislation. Its estimate is a weighted average of the projected per-person claims of those currently purchasing individual health insurance and the new entrants—those exercising their rights under the proposed legislation to purchase conversion coverage in the individual health insurance market, where the weights are given by the relative size of the two groups. For the latter group—those intending to purchase conversion coverage—the availability of such health insurance is clearly an advantage over the current situation. For the former group—those who currently purchase health insurance in the individual market—HIAA claims that the proposed legislation will make their situation worse.

In particular, HIAA has claimed that premiums for those *currently purchasing individual health insurance* will rise by the percentage implied by its methodology for computing the average increase in individual premiums (22.1 percent using the HIAA underlying figures; or 5.7 percent using its methodology, but our new and improved figures). This claim involves a crucial additional analytic assumption. The premiums for those currently purchasing individual health insurance will rise only by the percentages implied by the analysis in the previous chapter if insurance companies selling individual health insurance policies treat those exercising the conversion rights guaranteed by the proposed legislation the same as they treat those currently purchasing health insurance.

THE PROPOSED LEGISLATION

Nothing in the proposed federal legislation would require insurance companies to treat all individuals the same. The proposed legislation merely requires that those insurance companies that sell health insurance to any individuals also offer to sell health insurance to those who meet the proposed legislation's requirements: that they have been continuously insured as part of a group health insurance plan for 18 months and that they have no other potential source of group health insurance (e.g., the employer of another family member or COBRA continuation coverage). The proposed legislation has no requirement about the premium at which the insurance must be offered.   Thus, according to the proposed federal legislation, insurance companies could price such conversion coverage separately from their current individual insurance policies. In particular, they could set premiums for their conversion policies to cover all of the claims (and other costs, plus normal operating profits) of the conversion policies. Alternatively, they could set premiums for conversion coverage based on preexisting conditions and current health status. In either case, there would be no effect on the premiums of those currently buying individual health insurance. As HIAA states (Wildsmith, 1996):

> Clearly, if you assume carriers will be able to charge substantially higher premiums for this population, then you have succeeded in guaranteeing access to a policy that is unaffordable to most consumers. This is a rather hollow guarantee.

THE ROLE OF THE STATES

This scenario is, however, not the correct one for evaluating the likely effects of the proposed legislation. Both the proposed legislation and the HIAA analysis[1] assign to the states the role of regulating the premiums for the new conversion policies.

---

[1]HIAA (1995) states: "The proposal would not specify the rating rules applicable to premiums for coverage obtained under the new portability rules, leaving such regulation to the states."

When considering the effect of state regulation, we can divide the states into three groups (see Table 4 for a state-by-state analysis):[2]

1. Ten states already require guaranteed issue[3] (and regulate rates) in the individual insurance market (or some regulation such as guaranteed issue with similar effect).[4] For individuals in those states, the proposed federal legislation conversion requirement is redundant and would have no effect on premiums.

2. Thirty-six states place no limitation on individual rates. In those states, competition will be expected to force insurance companies to treat conversion policies separately from current individual insurance policies. Again, the premium for those currently purchasing individual insurance would not be affected by the proposed federal legislation.

3. Five states do not currently require guaranteed issue but have some rate regulation (limiting the variability of rates in the individual insurance market).[5] In these states, the proposed federal legislation would have some effect on premiums of those currently purchasing individual health insurance.

---

[2] Other analyses of the impact of state regulation on the effects of the proposed legislation on the premiums of those currently purchasing individual insurance include AAA (1996b) and Hustead (1996). General discussions of state regulation of insurance markets include General Accounting Office (GAO) (1995), Mollica (1995), Findlay and Loranger (1995), BlueCross BlueShield Association (BCBS) (1995), Communicating for Agriculture (1995).

[3] These laws require carriers to offer coverage to all individuals regardless of their health status or claims experience.

[4] Hawaii has a universal system. The following 11 states have "guaranteed issue": Idaho, Iowa, Kentucky, Maine, New Hampshire, New Jersey, New York, Ohio, Utah, Vermont, and Washington. With the exception of Ohio, all of these states also have rate regulation. Even among these states, only New Jersey and New York do not allow at least some adjustments for age. Even when fully phased in, the allowable bands for age are quite wide: Kentucky 3:1, Maine 1.5:1, New Hampshire 3:1, North Dakota 5:1, Vermont 1.5:1, and Washington 3.75:1.

[5] Louisiana (1.2:1 for factors other than demographics), Minnesota (1.2:1 for factors other than age; 1.4:1 for age), North Dakota (5:1 for age and industry), South Carolina (1.4:1 for factors other than demographics), and West Virginia (no more than 30 percent above current rates).

Table 4

State Insurance Regulation, High-Risk Pools, and BCBS Open Enrollment

State	State pop.	GI-yes RR-yes	GI-yes RR-no	GI-no RR-yes	GI-no RR-no	BCBS	HRP	Waiver	Waiver or GI
Alabama	4.3			√		√		√	√
Alaska	0.6				√		√	√	√
Arizona	4.2				√				
Arkansas	2.5				√		√	√	√
California	31.6				√		√	√	√
Colorado	3.7				√		√	√	√
Connecticut	3.3				√		√	√	√
Delaware	0.7				√				
District of Columbia	0.6			√		√		√	√
Florida	14.2				√		√		
Georgia	7.2				√				
Hawaii	1.2				√		√	√	√
Idaho	1.2	√							√
Illinois	11.8				√		√	√	√
Indiana	5.8				√		√	√	√
Iowa	2.8	√					√	√	√
Kansas	2.6				√		√	√	√
Kentucky	3.9	√							√
Louisiana	4.3		√				√	√	√
Maine	1.2	√							√
Maryland	5.0			√		√		√	√
Massachusetts	6.1			√		√		√	√
Michigan	9.5			√		√		√	√
Minnesota	4.6		√				√	√	√
Mississippi	2.7				√		√	√	√
Missouri	5.3				√		√	√	√
Montana	0.9				√		√	√	√
Nebraska	1.6				√		√	√	√
Nevada	1.5				√				
New Hampshire	1.1	√				√		√	√
New Jersey	7.9	√				√		√	√
New Mexico	1.7				√		√	√	√
New York	18.1	√							√

Table 4—continued

State	State pop.	GI-yes RR-yes	GI-yes RR-no	GI-no RR-yes	GI-no RR-yes	BCBS	HRP	Waiver	Waiver or GI
North Carolina	7.2				√				
North Dakota	0.6			√			√	√	√
Ohio	11.2		√						√
Oklahoma	3.3				√		√	√	√
Oregon	3.1				√		√	√	√
Pennsylvania	12.1				√	√		√	√
Rhode Island	1.0				√	√		√	√
South Carolina	3.7			√			√	√	√
South Dakota	0.7				√				
Tennessee	5.3				√		√	√	√
Texas	18.7				√				
Utah	2.0	√					√	√	√
Vermont	0.6	√				√		√	√
Virginia	6.6				√	√		√	√
Washington	5.4	√					√	√	√
West Virginia	1.8			√					
Wisconsin	5.1				√		√	√	√
Wyoming	0.5				√		√	√	√
Totals		10	1	5	35	11	27	37	42

SOURCES: BCBS (1995), Communicating for Agriculture (1995), Hustead (1996).

NOTES: Column headings use the following abbreviations:

State pop.: State population (in millions).

GI: Guaranteed issue (in the individual insurance market).

RR: Any rate regulation (in the individual insurance market).

BCBS: State's BCBS program has open enrollment for individual insurance policies.

HRP: State has a high-risk pool (which is active and not closed to new entrants; some such pools would probably need to offer a wider range of health plans and/or ease their preexisting condition rules to qualify for a waiver).

Waiver: State has a policy (BCBS or HRP) such that it could qualify for a waiver from the proposed federal legislation (if it applied for the waiver and perhaps if it changed its HRP rules).

Waiver or GI: State has a policy (BCBS or HRP) such that it could qualify for a waiver from the proposed federal legislation (if it applied for the waiver and perhaps if it changed its HRP rules) or it already has GI in the individual insurance market such that the proposed federal legislation is redundant.

Even in the five states that regulate health insurance premiums in the individual insurance market (and do not already have guaranteed issue and presumably in any other states that might adopt rate regulation in response to the proposed federal legislation), the effect of the proposed federal legislation is likely to be much smaller than that implied by the HIAA methodology for the change in average premium in the individual insurance market (i.e., our smaller RAND estimates).

1. Our RAND-Best estimate would be appropriate only in a state with pure community rating. Currently, all five of the states with rate regulation but not guaranteed issue in the individual market do not have pure community rating. They each allow some variation with the age of the insured individual.[6] All but North Dakota allow at least some rate banding for health status. The larger are these *rate bands*, the smaller is the appropriate estimated effect relative to our revised estimate based on the HIAA methodology.

2. The interaction of the proposed federal legislation with the state high-risk pools may further lower the effects. If states allow expensive conversion policies to be shifted to the high-risk pool, then the average claims cost will be even lower.

3. States with high-risk pools (including four of the five states with rate regulation but not guaranteed issue) could apply for waivers from the proposed federal legislation.[7] If the waiver was granted, the proposed federal legislation would have no effect.

----

[6]The current COBRA population appears to be disproportionately older (see Flynn, 1992). This age selection probably explains some of the higher cost of COBRA coverage relative to either the health insurance groups that they left (i.e., their previous employer) or those currently purchasing individual health insurance. Inasmuch as states allow age rating of individual insurance premiums, the relevant relative claims cost is within age groups.

[7]The Committee Report (1995, p. 34) on the bill states: "State reforms of the individual market will apply [i.e., will satisfy the waiver requirement] . . . if they achieve the objectives of the legislation." That report continues stating that it is the intention of this waiver provision "to provide substantial leeway for States to craft individualized solutions." Among the provisions listed as potentially satisfying the waiver requirements are high-risk pools and BCBS's open enrollment (without regard to health status or claims history) for individual policies.

Thus, *even in states with binding rate regulation*, our revised estimate using the HIAA methodology is likely to overestimate the increase in premiums for those currently buying health insurance.

Finally, the correct effect on the *national average premium* in the individual insurance market is even smaller. It is the weighted average of this effect in states with binding rate regulation and zero. Since less than six percent of the nation's population lives in states with a non-zero effect, the national effect will be much smaller than that implied by our estimates using the HIAA methodology. Weighting by the share of the population in states without binding rate regulation and down weighting the HIAA methodology estimates for less than pure community rating imply a national estimate of under 0.2 percent.

The exact results will depend on state reactions. It seems likely (see for example AAA, 1996b; Wildsmith, 1996) that not all states that could apply for waivers would (nor would all states with preexisting-condition limitations on their current high-risk pools remove them). Furthermore, it seems likely that in response to the proposed federal legislation and ongoing initiatives of the National Association of Insurance Commissioners (NAIC) more states will adopt some form of rate regulation for the individual health insurance market (Findlay and Loranger, 1995; Mollica, 1995; AAA, 1996b). Again, much of the resulting state regulation is likely to impose rate bands (not a single premium) and/or allow age rating. Depending on how many states do not apply for waivers, how many states adopt rate regulation, and the details of the rate regulation, the total effects could be larger than the under 1 percent estimate implied by the current regulatory environment; but effects on national average premiums of even half that implied by our revised estimates based on the HIAA methodology seem unlikely.

Chapter Five

CONCLUSION

This report has presented revised estimates of the effect of the proposed federal Health Insurance Reform Act of 1995 (S. 1028). The revised estimates maintain the basic HIAA methodology but substitute newly computed estimates of the key figures used therein. Because of the lack of appropriate data, HIAA was able to use only nonrepresentative data from health insurance industry sources, but our newly computed estimates are based on specially designed tabulations of nationally representative panel data from the U.S. Bureau of the Census.

While HIAA's estimates showed an increase in the average premium for individual health insurance under the proposed legislation of over 20 percent (22.1 percent in HIAA I), our recalculations imply estimates a quarter of that size (5.7 percent for RAND I corresponding to HIAA I). Alternative, and we think more plausible, assumptions yield an estimate of a 2.3 percent increase in the average premium for individual health insurance. But both of these low figures are likely too high because of several conservative assumptions in generating the underlying tabulations and figures.

Consideration of the nature of state regulation implies that even this lower, more plausible estimate is too high. The proposed federal legislation has no rate regulation. Even in states with rate regulation (or that will adopt rate regulation in response to the proposed federal legislation), the HIAA methodology would be appropriate only with pure community rating, i.e., under regulation that allows for no variation in rates for age or other factors. No state that does not also require guaranteed issue currently has such stringent rate regulation.

Instead, those states that have rate regulation allow adjustments for age and usually for other factors. As the number and range (i.e., the rate bands) of such adjustments increase, the effect on the premium of those currently purchasing health insurance declines from that implied by the HIAA methodology (e.g., the HIAA-RAND or RAND-Best estimates).

Finally, even these effects are applicable only in a small minority of states (under current state regulations, only five). There will be no effect in states without rate regulation, or in states that already have guaranteed issue in the individual insurance market. Since they already have either a high-risk pool or an insurer of last resort (i.e., if the state's BCBS offers open enrollment for its individual insurance), most of the remaining states could receive a waiver. With a waiver, the proposed federal legislation would have no effect.

The phase-in period of these estimates will be several years. In a market with recent premium increases of well over 5 percent per year, the long-run effect of this legislation—a few percentage points at most—is likely to be undetectable.

The original HIAA estimate of premium increases of over 20 percent for those currently buying health insurance in the individual health insurance market understandably induced many to reconsider the desirability of such a conversion right. By comparison, our preferred range of estimates of 5.7 percent to under 1 percent suggests that likely premium increases for those currently buying health insurance in the individual insurance market provide less reason to oppose the proposed legislation.

TECHNICAL ISSUES IN THE ESTIMATION
OF KEY FIGURES

This technical appendix provides more details on the assumptions, computations, and results underlying the estimates discussed in the body of the report. It begins with an overview of the CPS database and the derivation of the population estimates from the *EBRI Databook* (EBRI, 1995). It then provides an overview of the main SIPP database, followed by detailed descriptions of the overall "previous insurance" rates and results stratified by firm size and job tenure.

THE CURRENT POPULATION SURVEY

The basic data for both the original estimates and our reestimates of the total populations (in the individual health insurance market and in the COBRA and sub-COBRA-coverage components of the employer-sponsored market) are derived from the March Demographic Supplement to the CPS. This component of the CPS is a large nationally representative annual survey (of approximately 55,000 households) conducted by the U.S. Bureau of the Census. These questions nominally refer to the previous calendar year. Most analysts interpret responses as referring to status as of the interview date (EBRI, 1996).

The HIAA I analysis was based on the 1994 CPS. Since its analysis, the 1995 CPS data were released. These data are preferred not only because they are more recent, but also because they are based on a revised and more detailed set of health insurance questions (EBRI, 1996). These questions appear to have had the twin effects of increasing the number of people reporting employer-based coverage and lowering the number of people reporting individual coverage. In addition, the new questions appear to have substantially improved the reporting of children's health insurance.

Size of the Individual Market

The size of the individual market is traditionally computed from the CPS totals for the private (nongovernmental) insurance not provided through an employer. EBRI (1996) refers to this as "other private" health insurance coverage and defines it as

> Individual or group coverage not offered through an individual's current or former employer or union. This category consists primarily of individual purchased health insurance.

Some of these individuals, however, are not covered through the individual market. HIAA (1995) states

> Note that published estimates of the size of the individual market are generally estimates of non-governmental, non-employer-based coverage. Such estimates include association group policies, specified disease policies, hospital indemnity policies, etc.

HIAA's estimates are based on insurance industry sources, and its computations use an estimate of 10.4 million lives in the individual market (counting both the name on the policy and his or her dependents).

Our estimate of 13.2 million lives covered in the individual insurance market is computed using the more recent CPS data and an alternative partitioning of the "other private coverage" group between true individual insurance and other policies. In particular, our figure is computed as 80 percent of the 16.4 million of those with "other private coverage" in the 1995 CPS data (EBRI, 1996; calculated from the March 1995 CPS). The 80 percent figure is the most conservative estimate (implying the largest effect) from the American Academy of Actuaries range of values (AAA, 1996b).[1]

---

[1]AAA (1996b, A-3, note 10) states

Size of the COBRA and Sub-COBRA Insurance Markets

The HIAA I figures for the number of covered lives in the COBRA and sub-COBRA-insurance markets are derived from EBRI estimates based on the 1994 CPS (EBRI, 1995). The relevant table is reproduced here as Table A.1.

The HIAA I figures are 110 million and 30 million covered lives in the COBRA and sub-COBRA-insurance markets, respectively. It is not clear how HIAA derived its figures. The total of 140 million (110 million + 30 million) is close to the "total employer coverage" figure. To get close to the 30 million figure for the sub-COBRA-insurance market, however, we must add all of the "self-employed," all of the "nonworker," and all of the "private sector," "fewer than 10," and "20–24" covered lives (26.5 = 7.4 + 4.3 + 7.3 + 7.5).

Even ignoring the rounding to the closest 10 million (an increase of 13 percent), this calculation does not seem to estimate the right concept. First, some portion of covered lives in the 10–24 employees category actually have 20–24 employees and are thus COBRA-coverage eligible. Second, the "self-employed" are probably not appropriately treated as part of the population at risk. Many of them are in fact buying individual insurance through their self-employed firm (we do not add them back into our estimates of the size of the individual insurance market; doing so would further lower our estimate). They presumably have lower turnover than the employees (for whom we quote turnover rates below). If health insurance was crucial to them (and as long as they do not go bankrupt), they could stay in their current "self-employed" status.

Finally, note that these estimates of the sub-COBRA-insurance market are themselves probably too high. Because of data limitations in the CPS, the classification is by the "firm size of family head's em-

---

We use the word "individual" in this context to refer not only to the true legal definition of a policy owned by an insured individual (and his or her family), but also to those individuals who are insured through identical criteria, such as loosely defined discretionary group trusts and associations. For this estimate, we assumed that between 80% and 90% of those privately insured in the U.S. by means other than through the employer would fall into this category. We assumed that S.1028 would apply to both the true legal definition of private individual health insurance and the looser definition as we define it.

Table A.1

Health Insurance by Firm Size

(Based on 1994 CPS, Nonelderly Population with Selected Sources of Health Insurance, by Work Status and Firm Size of Family Head's Employer,[a] 1993)

Firm Size of Family Head's Employer	Total	Total Private	Employer Coverage			Type of Insurance			No Health Insurance Coverage
			Total	Direct	Indirect	Other Private	Total Public	Medicaid	
Total	226.2	157.7	137.4	72.0	65.4	20.8	36.3	28.9	40.9
Self-employed	17.8	12.1	7.4	3.3	4.1	4.8	1.2	0.8	4.9
Wage and salary workers	181.1	138.7	125.7	65.8	60.0	13.4	19.7	14.7	29.7
Public sector	32.8	28.3	26.3	14.0	12.4	2.1	3.1	1.6	3.0
Private sector	148.3	110.3	99.4	51.8	47.6	11.3	16.5	13.1	26.7
Fewer than 10	19.1	9.8	7.3	3.8	3.6	2.5	3.3	2.8	6.5
10–24	14.8	9.0	7.5	3.9	3.6	1.6	2.2	1.7	4.3
25–99	22.5	15.8	14.2	7.5	6.7	1.6	2.6	2.2	4.9
100–499	25.5	19.8	18.2	9.4	8.8	1.7	2.6	2.0	4.0
500–999	9.6	8.0	7.4	3.8	3.6	0.6	0.8	0.7	1.2
1,000 or more	56.8	48.1	44.9	23.4	21.4	3.3	5.0	3.7	5.8
Nonworker	27.3	6.9	4.3	2.9	1.4	2.6	15.4	13.4	6.3
				(percentage within coverage categories)					
Total	100.0%	100.0%	100.0%	100.0%	100.0%	100.0%	100.0%	100.0%	100.0%

SOURCE: Sarah C. Snider and Paul Fronstin, "Sources of Health Insurance and Characteristics of the Uninsured, Analysis of the March 1994 Current Population Survey," EBRI Issue Brief, no. 158 (see EBRI, 1995, Table 8.13).

NOTE: Details may not add to totals because individuals may receive coverage from more than one source.

[a]Family head is defined as the family member with the greatest earnings; all other family members with earnings are designated as secondary workers.

ployer." The appropriate concept for the COBRA/sub-COBRA-insurance distinction is the firm size of the individual providing the health insurance.   This partially explains the anomalous last row "nonworker" (nonworkers who nevertheless receive insurance from an employer; some of them have insurance from a previous employer, e.g., COBRA coverage). These are households in which someone other than the household head (e.g., a spouse or adult child of the head) is providing health insurance to some (perhaps) all household members. Rather than treating all of these individuals as being in the sub-COBRA-insurance market (as the HIAA estimate appears to do), it is probably preferable at least to spread these "nonworkers" according to the shares of those individuals for whom we have a firm size (at least of the household head). Our preferred estimate (see below), implies that this would put less than 10 percent of these "nonworkers" into the sub-COBRA-insurance market.

More generally, these EBRI tabulations probably overstate the number of covered lives in the sub-COBRA-insurance market. Larger employers are more likely to offer insurance. Even among employers offering group health insurance, on average, smaller firms are charged higher health insurance premiums (because of the higher costs of selling to smaller firms) and pay a smaller share of the premium themselves (for the individual or for dependents)—i.e., they require larger contributions from the employee. Thus, when there are two working individuals in the household, it will be more likely that the individual working at the larger firm will provide the insurance. This will not always be the head of household. These considerations imply that simply tabulating the size of the employer of the head of household is likely to overstate the size of the sub-COBRA-insurance market (again implying that our estimated effects are too large).[2] Further research on the size of this bias is indicated.

The HIAA II figures for employment-based insurance are drawn from the AAA (1996b) figures, which are based on the 1995 CPS. The HIAA

---

[2]The American Academy of Actuaries (1996b, p. A-2, note 7) states:

> It is assumed that between 40% and 60% of dependents of those family head small employer health insured lives are covered by large employer plans elsewhere, because, in general, a third or more of those who are offered a small employer insurance plan, opt not to participate.

II estimate continues to use the HIAA I estimate of 10.4 million covered lives.

Our estimates of the number of covered lives in the COBRA and sub-COBRA-insurance markets are derived from the 1995 CPS (a year later than the HIAA I estimates and using the improved question wording). The relevant table from EBRI (1996) is reproduced here as Table A.2.

We begin with a side computation. We need to allocate the people in the "10–24 workers" group. Those in firms of size 10–19 are not COBRA-coverage eligible. Those in firms of size 20–24 are COBRA-coverage eligible. Assuming a uniform distribution of firm sizes between 10 and 24 employees, we estimate that the shares of people in the 10–24 category who are actually in firms of size 10–19 and 20–24, respectively, are

$$56.9\% = \frac{145}{255} = \frac{10+11+\ldots+18+19}{10+11+\ldots+23+24} \text{ and}$$

$$43.1\% = \frac{110}{255} = \frac{20+21+\ldots+23+24}{10+11+\ldots+23+24}.$$

Using this approximation, we derive a rough approximation to the size of the sub-COBRA-insurance market as 10 percent of the wage and salary market (9.6 percent = 8.4 million covered lives in firms of less than 10 employees + 56.9 percent of the 7.7 million covered lives in firms of 10–24 employees / 133.5 million covered lives among wage and salary workers). Our computations ignore the self-employed. Many of them purchase individual insurance such that they would not be eligible for the conversion rights of the proposed federal legislation. Those that do purchase group insurance that would be covered by the proposed federal legislation have turnover rates sufficiently lower than that used in the computations (which is for employees) that the effect on the final estimate is likely to be negligible. Also, we have assumed that all of the "public sector" workers are in firms of 20 or more. We use this rough approximation to allocate the nonworkers among the COBRA and sub-COBRA-insurance markets.

Table A.2

Health Insurance by Firm Size

(Based on 1995 CPS, Nonelderly Population with Selected Sources of Health Insurance, by Work Status and Firm Size of Family Head's Employer, 1994)

Firm Size of Family Head's Employer	Total	Total Private	Type of Insurance			Other Private	Total Public	Medicaid	No Health Insurance Coverage
			Employer Coverage						
			Total	Direct	Indirect				
Total	228.1	162.3	145.9	75.1	70.8	16.4	37.2	28.7	39.4
Self-employed	17.3	12.5	8.2	3.7	4.5	4.4	1.3	0.8	4.0
Wage and salary Workers	185.0	143.0	133.4	68.4	64.9	9.6	21.4	15.4	29.4
Public sector	33.3	29.0	27.8	14.5	13.3	1.3	3.7	1.7	2.8
Private sector	151.7	114.0	105.6	53.9	51.7	8.4	17.7	13.7	26.6
Fewer than 10	20.1	10.7	8.4	4.1	4.2	2.4	3.4	2.8	6.7
10–24	14.8	9.0	7.7	3.9	3.8	1.3	2.2	1.8	4.2
25–99	23.1	16.3	15.1	7.8	7.3	1.2	3.0	2.5	4.8
100–499	25.6	20.2	19.1	9.8	9.3	1.1	2.7	2.2	3.7
500–999	10.0	8.2	7.9	4.1	3.9	0.3	1.0	0.7	1.2
1,000 or more	58.1	49.4	47.4	24.2	23.2	2.0	5.4	3.7	5.9
Nonworker	25.8	6.7	4.3	3.0	1.4	2.4	14.5	12.4	6.0
			(percentage within coverage categories)						
Total	100.0%	100.0%	100.0%	100.0%	100.0%	100.0%	100.0%	100.0%	100.0%

SOURCE: EBRI, 1996, Table 12.

Given these side computations, our figure for the total number of people in the 2–19 employees group (COBRA-coverage ineligibles) is 13.2 million. They are made up of the 8.4 million in the "fewer than 10" group, the 4.4 million from the "10–24" group who are actually in firms of size 10–19 (i.e., 56.9 percent of 7.7 million), and 0.4 million of the "nonworker" group (i.e., 9.6 percent of 4.3 million). The COBRA-insurance market is then the complement of this group, 124.5 million (the 133.4 million wage and salary workers, less the sub-COBRA-insurance market, plus the remaining share of the "nonworker" group).

These estimates are likely to be too conservative (implying an effect on premiums that is too large). We have excluded all of the self-employed from the individual insurance market and our only correction for the recording of firm size by household head rather than source of employment is for the "nonworkers." Correcting both of these problems would yield a smaller estimate.

Our estimates are lower than those of the American Academy of Actuaries (1996a). AAA estimates that there are 18.4 million (including 9 million dependents) individuals who "can claim that the head of their household works in employer sized programs of 20 or less—those not subject to COBRA" (please note that this appears to be an error, COBRA coverage does apply to groups of 20). AAA's estimate is higher because it includes the self-employed in the risk set (we exclude them). Note, however, that it does make a correction for the CPS's reporting of firm size of the household head, not the source of insurance. Using the AAA figure of 18.4 would raise our HIAA-RAND estimate about one percentage point.

SIPP DATABASE

The rest of our figures are derived from new tabulations from the Survey of Income and Program Participation conducted by the U.S. Bureau of the Census. The SIPP is a panel survey based on a nationally representative sample of the U.S. population. Individuals are interviewed every four months, covering a period of 24 to 36 months. A new panel is started approximately annually and includes about 20,000 households.

At each interview, the SIPP asks about employment and health insurance status during each of the four preceding months. The structure of the questions also makes it possible to identify individuals who have changed jobs, even when there is no intervening period without a job. Finally, the more recent waves used here specifically distinguish health insurance from a current versus that from a previous employer.

These SIPP-based estimates are, of course, only as good as the quality of the interviewing and the quality of the responses. In particular, our analyses assume that all COBRA coverage is reported as through a previous employer. Inasmuch as individuals do not view COBRA coverage as being through a previous employer, our estimates of the average COBRA-coverage duration per job leaver and the percentage of all job leavers exhausting COBRA coverage will be too small. Some individuals might misreport COBRA coverage because the employer does not contribute toward the COBRA-coverage premium or because the employer may instruct the former employee to make the COBRA-coverage payments to some third-party COBRA-coverage servicing agent (e.g., CobraServ, see below). Such misresponses are always possible in survey data. Note, however, that COBRA coverage is not like regular individual insurance. It has a clear statutorily determined limit, usually 18 months. Furthermore, the terms of the coverage are identical to those applying to employees (except that the former employee pays the entire cost). Thus, COBRA coverage does maintain a strong connection to the previous employer. These factors should mitigate underreporting due to misclassification of the source of insurance coverage.

The SIPP data are attractive for this analysis because they explicitly identify both the person in whose name the health insurance coverage is received and all individuals in the household covered by that policy. Unless otherwise noted, the tabulations that follow consider not simply the worker/job leaver (in whose name the policy is/was), but all "covered lives" (e.g., spouse and children).

The analyses reported here use the most recent available SIPP data. They analyze a dataset constructed by pooling data from the 1990 and the 1991 panels of the SIPP. The 1990 panel covers the period October 1989 to August 1992. The 1991 panel covers the period October 1990 to August 1993. These were periods of recession and recovery from a recession. These business-cycle phases should be kept in mind when interpreting the results.

Our sample includes individuals 16 to 64 years old at the time of the interview. The lower boundary is set by the youngest age at which individuals are asked the labor force questions. The upper boundary excludes retirees, who are eligible for Medicare. We also drop individuals who miss an interview, even if they are again interviewed at a subsequent date; but interviews before the missed interview are retained in the analysis file. Klerman (1992) shows that the bias in overall levels of health insurance coverage due to excluding those who missed interviews is negligible. The hazard models used below should also minimize the magnitude of any attrition bias.

Klerman (1992; see also Young, 1989) shows that the seam bias problem in the SIPP data is severe. Almost all transitions in employment and insurance status are reported to occur between the last period reported on in one interview and the first period reported on at the next interview (i.e., at the "seam" between the period reported on at one interview and the period reported on at the next interview). From the structure of the SIPP, we know that this is an artifact of the interview reporting period, not a strange periodicity of the true behavior. What appears to happen is that individuals propagate their current status back over all of the periods reported on at the interview. Below, we discuss how we adjust our analysis to account for this seam bias.

Computing Average Duration of COBRA Coverage and Percentage of Job Leavers Exhausting COBRA Coverage

HIAA I bases its estimates of COBRA-insurance take-up on *Spencer's Research Reports*: "Consistent with historic election percentage since 1990. *Spencer's Research Reports*: 329.04-01, 8/19/94." Presumably this is the information in the *EBRI Databook*, Table 8.17, p. 277 (shown as Table A.3). (See also the note to the table.)

Table A.3

COBRA Coverage
(Entitlement and Elections of Consolidated Omnibus Budget Reconciliation Act, Plan Years 1988–1992)

Plan Year	Employees Entitled to Coverage (as a % of Active Employees)	Employees Electing Coverage (as a % of Active Employees)	Employees Electing Coverage (as a % of Those Entitled)
1988	16.0	1.7	11.2
1989	9.2	2.6	28.5
1990	10.6	2.2	20.5
1991	12.1	1.6	13.2
1992	8.7	1.7	19.3

SOURCE: Employee Benefit Research tabulations from EBRI, 1995, Table 8.17, p. 277, of data from Spencer & Associates, 1993.

NOTE: The total number of employees counted in the 1993 survey was 3.1 million. A total of 204 companies responded to the survey.

HIAA I explains the source of its estimate of 20 percent for people who ever use COBRA insurance who exhaust it (use all 18 months) as follows:

> 10% of the unemployed have not had a job in the last 18 months (The Dynamics of Employment and Insurance, by Klerman and Rahman, RAND Corporation). We have assumed that those who expect only short-term unemployment are less likely to elect COBRA coverage.

This statement appears to refer to unpublished tabulations by Klerman and Rahman for HIAA in the early 1990s. Those tabulations explored time not employed and health insurance status (currently and on the previous job) of the currently unemployed. Related tabulations were published in Klerman and Rahman (1992). The tabulations were based on the 1984, 1985, and 1986 panels of the SIPP. Since the interviews for those panels did not distinguish health insurance provided by a current employer from health insurance provided by a previous employer, those tabulations cannot be used to delineate COBRA coverage (some of which is used after the individual is reemployed). Thus, the applicability of those tabulations to the percentage of COBRA-insurance participants who exhaust COBRA coverage is not clear.

For these figures for people who exhaust COBRA coverage, HIAA II uses the AAA assumptions. AAA (1996b, p. A-2, notes 2 and 3) explains these figures as

> 20% of lives becoming eligible for COBRA in any one year will elect the COBRA coverage (Generalized average of proportions reported over several years in surveys conducted by Spencer's Research Reports). . . . 22% to 28% of those individuals covered as a result of COBRA will continue until they exhaust the maximum benefit period of time allowed (18, 30, or 36 months).

No source is given for the latter statement.

We reestimate these figures directly from nationally representative individual data from the SIPP collected by the U.S. Bureau of the Census. Using other data sources, it appears to be easier to compute the COBRA-insurance take-up rate (among job leavers) and then to compute the number of months per person for taking up COBRA insurance or the percentage of those taking up COBRA insurance who exhaust it. Given data issues related to the SIPP (which we discuss in detail below), we believe that it is easier not to use this conditional computation structure. Instead, we attempt to estimate the number of months with COBRA coverage per job leaver (i.e., among all job leavers, whether or not they ever use COBRA insurance) and the percentage of all job leavers who exhaust COBRA coverage.

The idea underlying our estimate of the average COBRA-coverage duration and the percentage of job leavers exhausting COBRA coverage is straightforward. Ideally, with panel data we would simply follow all COBRA-coverage-eligible job leavers forward. To compute average COBRA-coverage durations per eligible person, we would simply count total years on COBRA coverage *per job leaver*. To compute the percentage of all job leavers exhausting COBRA coverage, we would use the fraction of all job leavers having COBRA coverage in month 18, but not in month 19.

Unfortunately, for several reasons, the estimation problem is considerably more complicated than is implied by the scheme of the previous paragraph. The issues and our solutions are as follows:

1. The SIPP panels are short (under three years) relative to the COBRA-coverage exhaustion time (a year and a half). Thus, for

anyone leaving his or her job after about the middle of the panel, we will not observe his or her behavior for the entire period for which the person is eligible for COBRA coverage (nor the point of time at which the person would exhaust COBRA coverage).

This problem suggests a hazard model. For every pair of months we observe, we compute the probability of having COBRA coverage in the second month of the pair, given that the person had COBRA coverage in the first month of the pair. Such a hazard model uses the information on every pair of observed months to estimate the overall probability of a spell of COBRA coverage lasting exactly M months. We then use these transition probabilities to simulate the probability of any history. This procedure is formally equivalent to a time-inhomogeneous first-order Markov transition model, where the time-inhomogeneity is in terms of months since leaving the job. We will see that most spells of "previous employer" are quite short; thus, this information on spells that we do not observe for the full 18 months is quite important in properly estimating time on COBRA coverage. These hazard-based estimates will therefore be more precise than those using only individuals observed for 18 months after leaving a job.

2. A person may apply for COBRA coverage up to several months after leaving the job. Thus, we cannot simply follow all the people who have COBRA coverage one month after leaving this job. Instead, we need a multistate hazard model. Throughout, we measure time in terms of duration since job leaving (not time in each state).

Specifically, we follow a person forward in the months after he or she leaves a job (from which the person received health insurance), until next entering a job providing health insurance (once entering a job providing health insurance, he or she becomes eligible for COBRA coverage from the new employer). We consider four mutually exclusive and exhaustive statuses:

   E-since leaving the job, has been employed, health insurance from current employer

and, among those who have not yet (through the reference month) held a job providing health insurance since leaving the reference job, there are three possible combinations of ever and current COBRA-coverage status:

N-never covered by COBRA

O-once covered, but not now covered, by COBRA

C-now covered by COBRA.

E, ever having held a job providing health insurance, is an absorbing status. For the purposes of the model, once a job leaver has ever become employed with health insurance from the current employer he or she is always in that status. When the person leaves this job providing health insurance, the model has a new job leaving event (and another observation at one month after job leaving).

For this set of statuses, for each month after leaving a job, we estimate the probability of changing from one of these four states to another state (based on all available pairs of months). We then use the estimates to simulate the probability of being in each status in each month.

3. The SIPP does not directly identify those on COBRA coverage. The interview collects the information that someone in the household had health insurance from a "previous employer" through a pair of questions. The first question asks about the source of health insurance, and the response would be "current or previous employer." The second question, added to the SIPP questionnaire with the 1990 wave (and determining which part of the SIPP we use), specifically asks "current" or "previous" employer. The interviewer would then get a list of the individuals covered through this relationship with a previous employer.

However, not everyone responding "previous employer" is in fact on COBRA coverage. Some firms offer at least short-term coverage for those terminating employment. Furthermore, as part of early retirement or severance plans, other firms offer long-term health insurance (often until Medicare eligibility at age 65). We cannot distinguish the COBRA-coverage policies from other previous employer coverage. We will proxy for COBRA-coverage exhaustion by all people who stop reporting COBRA coverage approximately at the point of COBRA-coverage exhaustion (see below). Again, this will be a conservative estimate (resulting in an overestimate of the effect of the proposed legislation).

4. In most months of the SIPP (see below), we cannot identify firm size and thus cannot distinguish COBRA-coverage eligibility from noneligibility. Again proceeding conservatively (leading to an overestimate of the effect of the proposed legislation), we assume that all "previous employer" coverage is from COBRA-coverage-eligible individuals. Specifically, from tabulations below, we estimate that 80 percent of job leaving events from insured jobs are to firms of size 25 or more. Thus, we divide the estimates of average COBRA-coverage duration and percentage exhausting COBRA coverage by 0.8.

Below, we will show limited evidence that in fact a considerable amount of "previous employer" coverage is from small firms (less than 25 employees). If so, then our estimates of time on COBRA coverage are too large. Below, we discuss other implications of this finding.

5. The problem of "seam bias" noted above implies that we would not expect all COBRA-coverage exhaustions to be reported as occurring exactly between month 18 and month 19. Seam bias suggests that many COBRA-coverage exhaustions would, in fact, be recorded between month 16 and month 17. We conservatively treat everyone who reports insurance from a "previous employer" at month 16, but not at month 20 as a COBRA-coverage exhaustion. Of course, some of these people would have dropped COBRA coverage even if COBRA coverage lasted forever, so this method is conservative (and leads to overestimates of the effect).

Table A.4 presents the results of this procedure. Among individuals leaving a job that provided employment-based group health insurance (by months since leaving the job), the second column gives the percentage of individuals reporting health insurance from a "previous employer." That percentage is highest in the month immediately after leaving the job, 25.05 percent. It falls quickly to 6.96 percent six months after leaving the job. Note also that two years later (after COBRA coverage for employment-related reasons is no longer available), 2.60 percent of job leavers still report health insurance from a "previous employer." This latter group is probably early retirees and others with coverage from a "previous employer" due to rights other than those resulting from COBRA (e.g., as part of an early retirement offer, etc.; Madrian, 1994).

Table A.4

Estimating COBRA-Coverage Spell Length

	Column A	Column B	Column C	Column D	Column E	Column F
Months	All Prev. Emp.	Emp. 20 +	p.d.f.	Adjust. p.d.f.	Avg. dur.	Total Months
1	25.05%	31.31%	8.86%	8.86%	1.5	0.1329
2	17.96%	22.45%	5.40%	5.40%	2.5	0.1349
3	13.64%	17.06%	2.58%	2.58%	3.5	0.0903
4	11.58%	14.47%	4.65%	4.65%	4.5	0.2093
5	7.86%	9.82%	1.12%	1.12%	5.5	0.0616
6	6.96%	8.70%	0.81%	0.81%	6.5	0.0526
7	6.31%	7.89%	0.28%	0.28%	7.5	0.0209
8	6.09%	7.61%	1.08%	1.08%	8.5	0.0920
9	5.23%	6.53%	0.37%	0.37%	9.5	0.0355
10	4.93%	6.16%	0.29%	0.29%	10.5	0.0301
11	4.70%	5.87%	−0.07%	−0.07%	11.5	−0.0082
12	4.75%	5.94%	0.77%	0.77%	12.5	0.0967
13	4.14%	5.17%	0.04%	0.04%	13.5	0.0057
14	4.10%	5.13%	0.04%	0.04%	14.5	0.0062
15	4.07%	5.08%	0.26%	0.26%	15.5	0.0408
16	3.86%	4.82%	0.53%	0.76%	42.0	0.3186
17	3.43%	4.29%	0.05%			
18	3.39%	4.24%	0.06%			
19	3.34%	4.18%	0.12%			
20	3.25%	4.06%	0.63%			
21	2.74%	3.43%	0.10%			
22	2.66%	3.32%	0.03%			
23	2.63%	3.29%	0.03%			
24	2.60%	3.26%				

NOTE: Columns are:

Months: Months since leaving job.

A: All Prev. Emp.: Percentage of all job leavers reporting continuation coverage (i.e., health insurance from a previous employer).

B: Emp. 20+: Same concept as "all prev. emp." for workers in the COBRA-insurance market under the assumption that all reported continuation coverage was from employers with 20 or more employees (i.e., the COBRA-insurance market).

C: p.d.f.: Probability that a continuation coverage will end in month M (using "Emp. 20+" estimates).

Table A.4—continued

D: Adjusted p.d.f.: Adjust p.d.f. to assume that anyone reporting a spell length of 17 to 20 months actually exhausted COBRA coverage, but anyone with spell lengths longer than 20 months was not on COBRA coverage.

E: Avg. dur.: Adjust duration for total length of those exhausting COBRA coverage in presence of the proposed legislation. Entry for 16 months (in italics) assumes COBRA-coverage exhaustion plus two years of conversion coverage ($42 = 18 + 24$ months).

F: Total months: Product of columns D and E. Summing down the column gives the average duration per COBRA-insurance-market job leaver (under the assumption that all reported continuation coverage is in the COBRA-insurance market and that all continuation spells lasting 20 months or less were actually COBRA insurance).

Simply from this column B, we can see that COBRA-coverage exhaustion is not that common. As noted earlier, because of concerns about seam bias, it is not appropriate to compare "previous employer" coverage in month 18 (the last month in which COBRA coverage should have been available) with "previous employer" coverage in month 19 (the first month in which COBRA coverage would not have been available because of COBRA-coverage exhaustion).

Instead, seam bias concerns suggest comparing coverage levels at the two seam months spanning the exhaustion point, 16 and 20 months. This difference 0.61 percent ($0.61 = 3.86 - 3.25$) is an approximate (see below) upper bound on people who exhaust COBRA coverage (and might therefore be eligible for and interested in purchasing conversion coverage). This is an overestimate because some of these people terminated continuation coverage for other reasons; e.g., they got a job offering health insurance, a spouse did, etc.

Furthermore, some of these people were not continuously covered by continuation coverage. Under COBRA, individuals can retroactively choose to buy COBRA coverage—even several months after leaving the job. These individuals, however, would not be eligible for the conversion policy. The proposed legislation requires continuous coverage in a group health plan. Some of the people without continuous coverage would have been induced by the proposed legislation to make their coverage continuous (so our estimates are slightly too low), others would not (so our estimates are too high).

The next several columns in Table A.4 present refinements of these simple calculations. The numbers in column B are too low. They assume that everyone was eligible for COBRA coverage. In fact, individuals in firms with under 20 employees are not eligible for COBRA coverage. Such individuals represent about 20 percent of all job leavers (see below). Column C adjusts the column B numbers to compute average months per COBRA-coverage-eligible person (not for all job leavers). It does so assuming that all "previous employer" coverage is from COBRA-coverage-eligible firms. Clearly this is an overestimate (see below). Nevertheless, it gives us an upper bound. To do the adjustment (and given the assumption), we can compute column C by dividing column B by the share of job leavers who are from COBRA-coverage-eligible firms; below we estimate that share at about 0.80. Dividing by 0.80 gives the third column; i.e., the percentage of individuals with COBRA-coverage spells lasting exactly M months. Thus, our preferred estimate (knowingly erring on the side of being too large) for the number of people exhausting COBRA-coverage is 0.76 percent of all individuals leaving employment covered under COBRA (0.76 = 4.82 − 4.06).

We now turn to trying to estimate the mean duration of COBRA-coverage collection per eligible person. Column D (labeled "p.d.f.") computes the probability of a job leaver reporting "previous employer" for exactly N months. The computation is performed by subtracting the percentage of people with "previous employer" coverage in month $N-1$, from the number in month N.

Following our concerns about seam bias, column E approximates the duration of continuation/conversion coverage given the reported duration of continuation coverage. It assumes that anyone reporting the last month of previous employer coverage was M, in fact was covered on average for $M+1$ months (assuming that half of the people actually found the job in the last month in which they reported "previous employer" and the other half paid for COBRA coverage for an additional month and were covered by some other source by the end of the month, again this will overestimate the effect). Finally, we assume that all individuals who report leaving at 17, 18, 19, or 20 months exhausted COBRA coverage and would have taken up conversion coverage for an average of 24/36 months (the HIAA I/HIAA II assumption), for a total for 42/54 months (42 months = 18 months + 24 months; or 54 months = 18 months + 36 months).

Summing down column F gives our estimate of continuation months per job leaver. Our estimate is that there are 0.1100/0.1176 years (less than a month and a half; SIPP I/SIPP II) of health insurance from a "previous employer" for every covered life associated with a job leaver. Given our take-up rate of any previous employer coverage of 31.31 percent, this implies an average duration on previous employer of 3.17 months (SIPP I, the SIPP II estimates are similar). If the take-up rate among COBRA-coverage eligible people is 20 percent, this implies an average COBRA-coverage duration of 4.96 months (= 0.1100 year × 12 months per year / 0.20 take-up rate).

Both the overall levels (per eligible individual) and the individual components (the take-up rates, time on COBRA coverage per take-up, and exhaustion rates per take-up) can be compared with industry sources. Our estimate that 31.31 percent of COBRA-coverage-eligible people take up the coverage is above that reported by *Spencer's Reports* (see EBRI, 1995, p. 277, Table 8.17). For 1988 to 1992, it estimates 11.2, 28.5, 20.5, 13.2, and 19.3, respectively. Our estimates correspond primarily to 1991, 1992, and 1993. The figure is also above the CobraServ estimate of 21 percent for work-related qualifying events for the period 1990–1991 (Flynn, 1993).

Note, however, that our estimate is too high because it assumes that all "previous employer" coverage, except that which lasts more than 20 months, is a result of COBRA coverage. In fact, some of these people were offered insurance from their previous employer for reasons other than COBRA coverage. In addition, this number assumes that there is no "previous employer" among those previously employed in the sub-COBRA-insurance market.

Our SIPP-based estimates for the duration of COBRA-coverage exhaustion and the duration of COBRA coverage are lower than those used in the other analyses of the proposed legislation (e.g., HIAA, 1995, 1996; AAA, 1996b). Note that the final column of Table A.4 computes the average duration on "previous employer" coverage, taking as a base those who were covered by "previous employer" in the month after leaving the job. This method yields an estimate of 4.0 months. This estimate is well below the CobraServ estimate of 7 months for "work-related qualifying events" (see Flynn, 1992).

Similarly, our estimate that only 0.76 percent (less than 1 percent) of those leaving a COBRA-coverage-eligible job exhaust COBRA coverage is higher than the CobraServ estimate of 2.01 percent (we compute this estimate as the product of the 19 percent take-up rate among those with a "work qualifying event" and the 11 percent exhaustion rate; see Table 11 and p. 113 in Flynn, 1992). This estimate is well below the 4 percent figure used by HIAA (the product of a 20 percent take-up rate and a 20 percent exhaustion rate) or the 5 percent figure used by AAA (the product of a 20 percent take-up rate and a 25 percent exhaustion rate).

At least two considerations could explain this divergence. First, the Spencer & Associates (1991) estimates are based on a small and selected sample. The source note in the *EBRI Databook* notes that these estimates are based on 204 responses to a mail survey representing 3.1 million covered lives. While this is a large number of covered lives, there is reason to believe that this is not a representative sample. In particular, large employers are more likely to be mailed such surveys and more likely to respond.

Similarly, the CobraServ results are likely to be unrepresentative. The CobraServ data represent the experiences of 6,625 firms with 1,344,461 employees. Employees tend to be from large firms. For example, 78 percent of CobraServ's data refers to individuals from firms of 401 or more employees. The comparable figures for all employer-provided insurance from the *EBRI Databook* (for a slightly different time-period and including those in firms below 20, who are not eligible for COBRA coverage—so the comparison is not exact) is only 38 percent.

Second, our estimates include all "previous employer" coverage, which ends at or before 20 months. Much of that coverage would not have been mandated by COBRA. In particular, while COBRA requires no contribution from the previous employer, some employers pay some part of the premium as part of a severance package or early retirement package. In addition, many insurance policies always cover some small number of months after an employee leaves a job. Such a policy would explain the sharp drop-off in coverage over the first six months. Presumably such coverage is not reported by Spencer & Associates (1991) or CobraServ as COBRA coverage. Nevertheless, here we would consider it as COBRA coverage.

Together, these considerations imply that our estimated percentage of months on COBRA coverage and our estimate of the percentage of individuals exhausting COBRA coverage are too large. If these estimates are too large, then our final computations overestimate the true effect on the individual market.

This estimate would be biased down if some of the short durations are "previous employer" coverage, but not COBRA coverage. Note, however, that our computations in the main analysis are based on months of continuation coverage among program-eligible people. Thus while spuriously including short non-COBRA-coverage "previous employer" spells will bias down the estimate of the average duration among those who use "previous employer" coverage, it will *bias up* (i.e., make too high) our estimates of months on "previous employer"/COBRA coverage per job leaver.

The SIPP data, however, are likely to be closer to the true values. They are based on nationally representative data; though, as noted above, there is likely to be some reporting of COBRA coverage as other private coverage. This underreporting of COBRA coverage is likely to be counterbalanced by the fact that we assume that all coverage through a previous employer is from COBRA-coverage-eligible firms (20 or more employees) and due to COBRA coverage itself.

The computations behind this calculation also allow us to describe what happens to job leavers. Among all individuals who leave an insured job, about half of them go immediately to another insured job (46 percent). A year after leaving a job, 70 percent of them have held a job offering health insurance; by two years, the comparable figure is 76 percent.

DIFFERENTIAL RESULTS BY FIRM SIZE

The basic SIPP interview does not include information on either firm size or job tenure. For the 1990 and 1991 panels, such information is available in a supplement to the second interview. In this section, we report results stratifying by firm size.

Unless otherwise noted, all of the results refer to individuals covered by employer-based group health insurance (in month 8, the last month reported on at interview 2). Job transitions and job tenure refer to the reference person supplying the insurance. That information is propagated to other individuals covered through him or her.

The SIPP breaks firm size at 25 workers (rather than the 20 employee cutoff in the COBRA legislation). Nevertheless, in what follows, we identify the "under 25 employees" group with the sub-COBRA-insurance market; and the 25 or more employees group with the COBRA-insurance market. In all of these tabulations (and those of the previous section), we exclude the self-employed.

We begin by considering job transition rates. The HIAA I estimates are for the COBRA-insurance market citing the non-nationally representative data from *Spencer's Research Reports*: "Consistent with historic percentages over the last six years. *Spencer's Research Reports*: 329.04-01, 8/19/94." The HIAA I estimate for the COBRA-insurance market is by assumption (without citation): "[R]eflecting higher turnover rates among smaller employers."

The HIAA II figures for job turnover are chosen to be identical to the AAA figures. AAA's (1996b) figures appear to be based on insurance industry estimates:

> 12% of lives (workers and dependents) insured with large employers who are required to offer COBRA will become eligible for COBRA as a result of group coverage expiring on those lives (p. A-1, note 1).

> 12% of those insured by small employers (less than 20 employees) will terminate or change employment. (It is assumed that the turnover rate is similar to that of large employer groups.) (p. A-2, note 7).

Mindful of seam bias, we compute turnover rates from the SIPP by considering the employment status at month 12 of those same individuals for whom we knew their firm size at month 8 (i.e., the last month reported on at the next interview). Four months later in the COBRA-insurance market, 94.48 percent of all covered lives are still associated with the same employer; 3.35 are with a different job, and 2.17 are not employed. We convert this four month turnover rate to an annual turnover rate by multiplying by three, yielding an annual turnover rate of 16.56 percent $(16.56 = 3 \times (100.00 - 94.48))$.

These estimates are higher than GAO's (1995, p. 4) estimates based on the CPS. GAO estimates that in 1993 11.5 million people with health insurance changed jobs, and that these individuals had 6.7

million dependents for a total of 18.2 million people. Our SIPP-based estimate of the equivalent numbers is 21.99 million. The SIPP estimate counts the number of job changes; the CPS estimate appears to count the number of people who changed jobs. The former is the appropriate concept for the HIAA calculations. In particular, our estimate of 3.10 million job leavers per year is higher than the GAO (1995, p. 4.1) estimate of 2 million individuals (it is not clear whether the GAO estimate refers only to workers, or also to their dependents; if the former, then the GAO and our SIPP estimates are close). Finally, note that this estimate is lower than those used by the American Academy of Actuaries (1996a,b). AAA estimates 12 percent turnover rates for both the COBRA and the sub-COBRA-insurance markets. Thus, its estimates are too low.

Similarly in the sub-COBRA-insurance market, four months later, 91.80 percent of covered lives are still associated with the same employer; 5.28 are at a different job, and 2.92 are not employed. We convert this four month turnover rate to an annual turnover rate by multiplying by three, yielding an annual turnover rate of 24.60 percent $(24.60 \times (100.00 - 91.80))$. Compared with the HIAA I estimate of 20 percent and the HIAA II/AAA estimate of 12 percent, our annual turnover rate is higher.

Only individuals with 18 months of continuous group health insurance coverage will be eligible for the conversion coverage. To get a rough estimate of how many people such a requirement will exclude, we computed the fraction of employees (and their covered lives) with 18 or more months of tenure. In the COBRA-insurance market, that figure is 83.53 percent. In the sub-COBRA-insurance market, that figure is 76.94 percent. There is considerable job turnover in the United States, even among individuals in jobs covered by health insurance.

The previous paragraphs describe the figures we use in our computations. Again, they are likely to imply too high a turnover rate and too large an impact on the individual insurance market. The reason is that individuals with 18 months or more of job tenure have lower job turnover rates than those with less than 18 months of job tenure. Our sample sizes get quite small for computing the stratified figures. Here we provide the weighted counts, but we do not use them in the final calculations. Among individuals in firms with less than 25 employees, the overall four-month same-job rate is 91.80. The rate for those with more than 18 months of job tenure is 93.55; the rate for those with less than 18 months of job tenure is 85.92. The corresponding annual turnover rates are 24.60 overall (as above), 19.35 for those with 18 or more months of tenure, and 42.24 for those with less than 18 months of job tenure. Thus, the estimates in the body of the report are too high because they give everyone in small firms the small-firm turnover rate. However, many of the people with the higher turnover rates will not have 18 continuous months of group health insurance and will therefore be ineligible for the conversion benefit.

In closing, we note "previous employer" coverage rates in the month after job leaving for different subsets of the population. These tabulations are limited to those who left a job between month 8 and month 9 (for which we know firm size)—in the COBRA-insurance market, overall 24.96; in the sub-COBRA-insurance market 21.33 (85 percent of the COBRA-insurance-market figure). Thus, the assumption that everyone reporting previous employer coverage is COBRA-coverage eligible is clearly in error. Again, this will make our estimates of the effects of the proposed legislation too large.

American Academy of Actuaries (AAA), "Providing Universal Access in a Voluntary Private-Sector Market," Washington, D.C.: Guaranteed Issue/Universal Access Working Group, Thomas J. Stoiber, Chairperson, February 20, 1996a.

American Academy of Actuaries (AAA), "Comments on the Effects of S. 1028 on Premiums in the Individual Health Insurance Market," Washington, D.C.: Guaranteed Issue/Universal Access Working Group, Thomas J. Stoiber, Chairperson, February 20, 1996b.

BlueCross BlueShield Association (BCBS), *State Legislative Health Care and Insurance Issues: 1995 Survey of Plans*, 1995.

Chen, Edwin, "Health Care Bill Travels Rugged Road of Reform," *Los Angeles Time*, February 4, 1996, p. A1.

Clymer, Adam, "Actuaries Fault Health Insurers' Stand on Bill," *New York Times*, February 6, 1996, p. A16.

Cochrane, John H., "Time-Consistent Health Insurance," *Journal of Political Economy*, Vol. 103, No. 3, 1995, pp. 445–473.

Communicating for Agriculture, *Comprehensive Health Insurance for High Risk Individuals: A State-by-State Analysis*, Ninth Edition, Bloomington, Minn., 1995.

Dewar, Helen, "Key GOP Senators Agree to Consider Limited Health Insurance Bill in Spring," *Washington Post*, February 7, 1996, p. A05.

Employee Benefits Research Institute (EBRI), *EBRI Databook*, Third Edition, Washington D.C., 1995.

Employee Benefits Research Institute (EBRI), "Sources of Health Insurance and Characteristics of the Uninsured: Analysis of the March 1995 Current Population Survey (with Appendix)," *EBRI Issue Brief*, Number 180, February, 1996.

Findlay, Steven, and Linda Loranger, "Health Reform 2: Should Congress Look to the States? *Business & Health*, (June) 1995, pp. 28–39.

Flynn, P., "Employment-Based Health Insurance: Coverage Under COBRA Continuation Rules," U.S. Department of Labor, Pension and Welfare Benefits Administration, *Health Benefits and the Workforce*, Washington, D.C.: Government Printing Office, 1992.

Flynn, P., "COBRA Qualifying Events and Elections, 1987–1991," *Inquiry*, Vol. 31 (Summer), 1994, pp. 214–220.

General Accounting Office (GAO), *Health Insurance Portability: Reform Could Ensure Continued Coverage for Up to 25 Million Americans*, letter report, 09/19/95, Washington, D.C., GAO/HEHS-95-257, 1995.

Gradison, Bill, "HIAA's Statement on Insurance Market Reform," Washington, D.C.: Subcommittee on Health, Committee on Commerce, U.S. House of Representatives, March 7, 1996.

Gray, Jerry, "Critics to Allow Vote on Health Insurance Bill, *New York Times*, February 7, 1996, p. A15.

Gruber, J., and B. C. Madrian, "Health Insurance and Job Mobility: The Effects of Public Policy on Job-Lock," *Industrial and Labor Relations Review*, Vol. 48, No. 1, 1994.

Gruber, J., and B. C. Madrian, *Non-Employment and Health Insurance Coverage*, Cambridge, Mass.: Massachusetts Institute of Technology and National Bureau of Economic Research, 1995.

Health Insurance Association of America (HIAA), *The Cost of Ending "Job Lock" or How Much Would Health Insurance Costs Go Up If*

"Portability" of Health Insurance Were Guaranteed? Preliminary Estimates—July 26, 1995, Washington, D.C.: HIAA, 1995.

Health Insurance Association of America (HIAA), *"Job Lock" Revisited or Examining the Cost of Group to Individual Portability Under S. 1028 Using Alternative Assumptions. How Would HIAA's Estimate of the Cost Change Using Selected Assumptions from the American Academy of Actuaries? March 7, 1996,* Washington, D.C.: HIAA, 1996.

Holtz-Eakin, D., "Health Insurance Provision and Labor Market Efficiency in the United States and Germany," R. Blank, ed., *Social Protection Versus Economic Efficiency: Is There a Trade-off?* Chicago, Ill.: University of Chicago Press, 1994.

Hustead, Edwin C., *Analysis of Individual Portability Provision of S. 1028 and Estimated Impact to Individual Market,* Washington, D.C.: Hay/Huggins Company, Inc., February 9, 1996.

Jouzaitis, Carol, "Tactic Stalls Popular Health-Care Bill; Handful of Senators Bottles Up Measure," *Chicago Tribune,* February 4, 1996, p. C1.

Klerman, J. A., "A Random Effects Approach to Attrition Bias in the SIPP Health Insurance Data," *Proceedings, Bureau of the Census Annual Research Conference, 1991,* pp. 335–351, 1991 (also available as RAND RP-118) .

Klerman, J. A., "Pitfalls of Panel Data: The Case of the SIPP Health Insurance Data," *Proceedings, The 1990's: A Decade of Decisions for Vital and Health Statistics, Public Health Conference on Records and Statistics, 1991,* pp. 36–39, 1992 (also available as RAND RP-111).

Klerman, J. A., and D. P. Goldman, "Job Loss Due to Health Insurance Mandates," *Journal of the American Medical Association,* Vol. 272, No. 7, pp. 552–556, 1994.

Klerman, J. A., and O. Rahman, "Employment Change and Continuation of Health Insurance Coverage." U.S. Department of Labor, Pension and Welfare Benefits Administration, *Health Benefits and the Workforce,* Washington, D.C.: Government Printing Office, 1992.

Long J. E., and M. D. Marquis, "COBRA Continuation Coverage: Characteristics of Enrollees and Costs in Three Plans," U.S. Department of Labor, Pension and Welfare Benefits Administration, *Health Benefits and the Workforce*, Washington, D.C.: Government Printing Office, 1992.

Madrian, B. C., "Employment-Based Health Insurance and Job Mobility: Is There Evidence of Job-Lock?" *Quarterly Journal of Economics*, Vol. 109, pp. 27–51, 1994.

Manning, W. G., et al., "Health Insurance and the Demand for Medical Care: Evidence from a Randomized Experiment," *American Economic Review*, Vol. 6, pp. 251–277, 1987.

Marquis, M. S., and S. H. Long, "Worker Demand for Health Insurance in the Non-Group Market," *Journal of Health Economics*, Vol. 14, pp. 47–63, 1995.

Marquis, M. S., and C. E. Phelps, "Price Elasticity and Adverse Selection in the Demand for Supplementary Health Insurance," *Economic Inquiry*, Vol. XXV, pp. 299–313, 1987.

Mollica, R. L., "State Health Reform," *Employee Benefits Journal*, (December) 1995, pp. 2–9.

Monheit, A. C., and P. F. Cooper, "Health Insurance and Job Mobility: Theory and Evidence," *Industrial and Labor Relations Review*, Vol. 48, No. 1, 1994, pp. 68–85.

Podgursky, M., and P. Swaim, "Health Insurance Loss: The Case of the Displaced Worker," *Monthly Labor Review*, April 1987, pp. 30–33.

Spencer & Associates, *Spencer's Research Reports on Employee Benefits*, Chicago, Ill.: Charles D. Spencer & Associates, 329.04-1, 1991.

Wildsmith, Tom, *Statement of the HIAA on the Cost of Group-to-Individual Portability*, presented before the Subcommittee on Health, Committee on Commerce, Washington, D.C.: U.S. House of Representatives, March 7, 1996.

Young, N., "Wave-Seam Effects in the SIPP," *Survey of Income and Program Participation Working Papers,* No. 8921, Washington, D.C.: U.S. Bureau of the Census, 1989.